All-Star

WORLD

David Scott

Beaver Books

A Beaver Book
Published by Arrow Books Limited
20 Vauxhall Bridge Road, London SW1V 2SA
An imprint of Random Century Group
London Melbourne Sydney Auckland
Johannesburg and agencies throughout the world

Beaver edition 1990
Reprinted 1990 (twice)
Text © David Scott 1990
The right of David Scott to be identified as the author of this work has
been asserted by him in accordance with the Copyright, Designs and
Patents Act, 1988.

Typeset by Goodfellow & Egan Ltd, Cambridge.
Editorial, design and production by Hart McLeod, Cambridge.
Made and printed in Great Britain by
Courier International Ltd, Tiptree, Essex

ISBN 0 09 973940 2

CONTENTS

For Isobel, Rachel and Rebecca Scott
in appreciation of their support
and encouragement.

Acknowledgements

The author would like to thank the following for their assistance with the preparation of this book:

Judith Black (Jay Bee Typing Services), Whitley Bay.

John Gibson (Sports Editor), Alan Oliver and Bob Moreland (Sports Writers) and Chris Hodgson, *Newcastle Evening Chronicle*.

John Kelly (John and Surtees Hair Base), Newcastle upon Tyne.

David and Julia McCreery.

INTRODUCTION

The Olympic Games provided world competition for footballers, but as the professional game grew throughout the world, FIFA, the organisation concerned with the administration of international football, wanted an equivalent competition for professional footballers.

FIFA, the Fédération Internationale de Football Association, had been formed in 1904. Nothing was done about a World Cup until the Antwerp Congress in 1920, when the idea was first put forward as a realistic proposal. After ten years of discussion and planning, Jules Rimet, the president of the French Football Association and FIFA, saw his dream become reality with the staging of the 1930 World Cup Finals in Uruguay.

The Uruguayans were celebrating a hundred years of independence and were the most enthusiastic of the five countries who applied to be host nation. The fact that they had been the champions of the previous two Olympics, in 1924 and 1928, clearly went very much in their favour when a decision was taken at the FIFA conference in Barcelona in 1929.

Out of respect for all the work Jules Rimet had done to launch the competition, FIFA decided to name the trophy the Jules Rimet Cup. It was solid gold, 32 cm high and weighed over 4 kg. Designed by French sculptor La Fleure, it cost 50,000 francs, a tidy sum in those days.

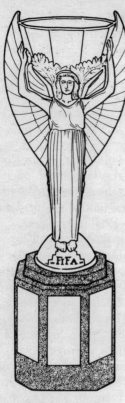

The Jules Rimet Cup   *The FIFA World Cup*

The Jules Rimet Cup was played for until 1970 when
Brazil, having won it three times, were allowed to keep
it for ever. The new FIFA trophy is solid gold, 36 cm
high and simply called the 'World Cup'. It was designed
by an Italian, Salvio Gazzaniga, and was selected from
53 entries. The World Cup cost £8000, was made in
18-carat gold and weighs about 4.54 kg (10 lb). It was
used for the first time in 1974.

Out of the thirteen competitions held to date, the host nation has taken the trophy five times: Uruguay, Italy, England, West Germany and Argentina. The stadia for World Cup Finals have become bigger and better as host countries have developed venues which will continue to provide facilities long after the competition is over. A special centre was built in Mexico City for the 1986 Finals to house the world's press and television; it had eight floors, four of them below ground level. All this was to cater for estimated viewing figures well in excess of one billion people.

FIFA has 150 associations affiliated and of these, 105 countries entered the qualifying rounds of the 1990 competition. This gives some indication of the massive increase in the popularity of the World Cup since thirteen teams first travelled from different parts of the world for that opening competition in Uruguay back in 1930.

— AMAZING FACT—

Brazil is the only country to have appeared in all thirteen Finals series. It was also the first to win the competition on three occasions – in 1958, 1962 and 1970 – and the team was presented with the Jules Rimet Trophy as a result.

THE STORY OF THE WORLD CUP

URUGUAY 1930

Five countries wanted to stage this first series: Holland, Italy, Spain, Sweden and Uruguay. Although a small country with a population of only two million, Uruguay had a proud footballing tradition and was eventually selected by FIFA. This decision may well have been taken because the host nation guaranteed all hotel and travelling expenses and even built a new stadium within eight months at Montevideo where the games could be played.

Thirteen countries participated, only four of which were European. This disappointed and disgusted the South Americans, but it seemed that the majority of European countries were not keen on the prospect of over two weeks' travel each way, the necessary mode of transport at that time being by sea and not by air as today. The teams were divided into three groups of three teams and one of four, as follows:

Pool 1
Chile, Mexico, Argentina and France

Pool 2
Bolivia, Brazil and Yugoslavia

Pool 3
Peru, Uruguay and Romania

Pool 4
Paraguay, United States of America and Belgium

The winners of each 'pool' progressed to straight, knock-out semi-final and final matches.

With the Austrians, Hungarians, Germans, Swiss and Czechs having refused to play, and the British not eligible because at that time they were not members of FIFA, the European teams which took part were by no means the best. The Romanians had entered on the instructions of their monarch, King Carol II, who even selected the national team! Uruguay were the clear favourites as reigning Olympic champions, having beaten Argentina in 1928. They had won the previous Olympic title by thrashing Yugoslavia 7–0 four years earlier. Home advantage was also in their favour.

Needless to say, the tournament was not without incident. In the first match the French goalkeeper was kicked in the head within the first ten minutes, and took no further part in the game. In the second match, against Argentina, the French were one goal down and their players all over the opposition, looking good for an equaliser, when the referee blew for time five minutes early. Both teams were called back from the dressing room to complete the match, but France had lost the impetus and went out of the competition.

There was a comical game between Argentina and

Mexico which finished 6–3, including five penalties. But Argentina's next game, against Chile, was nothing short of a brawl. The police were called on to the pitch to sort things out and cool a few of the hot-heads. Both semi-finals had identical scores of 6–1, with Uruguay and Argentina reaching the Final. It may seem surprising that the USA managed third place, when it is generally believed that soccer in the States did not really take off until well after the Second World War. Apparently, though, their team comprised very big men with terrific stamina and great enthusiasm.

The first World Cup Final became a re-run of the 1928 Olympic final with the champions, Uruguay, facing their neighbours and rivals Argentina. Thousands of Argentinians had crossed the River Plate on chartered packet boats to support their team, and they were searched for weapons outside the stadium. Even before the start there was an argument about which match-ball to use. Referee 'Long John' Langenus, wearing a cap and plus-fours, came on to the field with a ball under each arm. It was agreed to play with one in each half, an Argentinian ball in the first and Uruguay's in the second. Although the home side were trailing 2–1 at half-time, they scored three goals in the second half to secure a victory that was celebrated in Montevideo long into the night.

The Uruguayan players were acclaimed as national heroes, and the day following the Final was declared a public holiday. The winners had the trophy, a 100,000 capacity stadium, and a team that had completed a hat-trick of victories in the world arena. The others returned home defeated, but richer by far. The World Cup was on its way to becoming the focus of international footballing interest and enthusiasm, which it remains today.

Results

Pool 1

France 4, Mexico 1   Chile 1, France 0
Argentina 1, France 0   Argentina 6, Mexico 3
Chile 3, Mexico 0   Argentina 3, Chile 1

	P	W	D	L	F	A	Pts
Argentina	3	3	0	0	10	4	6
Chile	3	2	0	1	5	3	4
France	3	1	0	2	4	3	2
Mexico	3	0	0	3	4	13	0

Pool 2

Yugoslavia 2, Brazil 1   Brazil 4, Bolivia 0
Yugoslavia 4, Bolivia 0

	P	W	D	L	F	A	Pts
Yugoslavia	2	2	0	0	6	1	4
Brazil	2	1	0	1	5	2	2
Bolivia	2	0	0	2	0	8	0

Pool 3

Romania 3, Peru 1   Uruguay 4, Romania 0
Uruguay 1, Peru 0

	P	W	D	L	F	A	Pts
Uruguay	2	2	0	0	5	0	4
Romania	2	1	0	1	3	5	2
Peru	2	0	0	2	1	4	0

Pool 4

United States 3, Belgium 0   Paraguay 1, Belgium 0
United States 3, Paraguay 0

	P	W	D	L	F	A	Pts
United States	2	2	0	0	6	0	4
Paraguay	2	1	0	1	1	3	2
Belgium	2	0	0	2	0	4	0

Semi-finals

Argentina 6   **United States 1**
Monti, Scopelli, Stabile (2),   Brown
Peucelle (2)

Uruguay 6	Yugoslavia 1
Cea (3), Anselmo (2), Iriarte	Seculic

Final

Uruguay 4	Argentina 2
Ballesteros; Nasazzi (capt.), Mascheroni; Andrade, Fernandez, Gestido; Dorado, Scarone, Castro, Cea, Iriarte.	Bottasso; Della Torre, Paternoster; Evaristo, J., Monti, Suarez; Peucelle, Varallo, Stabile, Ferreira (capt.), Evaristo, M.

SCORERS	SCORERS
Dorado, Cea, Iriarte, Castro (HT 1/2)	Peucelle, Stabile

ITALY 1934

The second World Cup was played in Italy, one of the unsuccessful applicants for the prestige of staging the 1930 series. It had taken eight FIFA meetings to confirm this venue. Now it was realised that the competition could not be confined to a single city, nor to a country without huge resources. The holders, Uruguay, declined to defend their title, the only reigning champions ever to do so. They did not participate for at least two reasons, one being their annoyance that so few European teams had visited Montevideo four years earlier, and another the fact that their players were on strike!

To reduce the initial thirty-two entrants to a more manageable sixteen, a qualifying tournament was held. Dispensing with the pool system used in the previous Finals, a knock-out system was employed. As a result, half of the entrants played only a single game. Indeed, the Mexican team, who had travelled all the way to Rome to play their qualifying eliminator with their neighbours the United States, did not participate in the Finals at all.

12

Twelve of the sixteen finalists were from Europe – Austria, Belgium, Czechoslovakia, France, Germany, Holland, Hungary, Italy, Romania, Spain, Sweden and Switzerland; one from Africa – Egypt; one from North America – USA; and only two from South America – Brazil and Argentina.

It was known that Italy had the advantages of stamina, power and also home support. The Czechs had skill and subtlety, playing a short passing game. The Austrian 'Wunder Team' were also a favoured side, but were to find the heavy conditions in the later stages unsuited to their style of play. Although the Germans were well organised, they did not have the finishing power of the other European favourites.

Both South American countries were eliminated in the first round; Argentina had left their star players at home and were soon to face further defections to wealthy Italian clubs. The semi-finals saw Italy playing and beating Austria by a single goal, while the Czechs outplayed the physical Germans to win 3–1.

The Final, played in Rome before a below-capacity crowd of 55,000, was a good match. When the Czechs took the lead twenty minutes from the end through Puc, Italy seemed to have lost their chance of victory, especially when the ball rebounded off an Italian goal-post a few minutes later. Unfortunately for the Czechs, the Italians equalised in the last few minutes, Orsi unleashing a bender which curled into the net, taking the Final into extra time. The strength and stamina of the Italians held them in good stead, and they were further spurred on by a fanatical crowd which went delirious with delight when they scored the winner through Schiavio. The Czechs, whose enthusiasm and accuracy had been superior to those of the Italians throughout, had not been able to keep up the pace.

All in all, the second World Cup tournament had been successful, and interest in the competition had been considerable. The Italians made a sizeable profit and the number of participants looked encouraging for the future. Apart from the rough play, the main black spot was the sub-standard refereeing which contributed to some regrettable behaviour on the part of the players. One referee was even suspended from officiating by his own Association after his terrible performance in one game.

Results

First round

Italy 7, United States 1	Spain 3, Brazil 1
Czechoslovakia 2, Rumania 1	Switzerland 3, Holland 2
Germany 5, Belgium 2	Sweden 3, Argentina 2
Austria 3, France 2	Hungary 4, Egypt 2

Second round

Germany 2, Sweden 1	Italy 1, Spain 1
Austria 2, Hungary 1	Italy 1, Spain 0 (replay)
Czechoslovakia 3, Switzerland 2	

Semi-finals

Czechoslovakia 3	**Germany 1**
Nejedly (2), Krcil	Noack
Italy 1	**Austria 0**
Guaita	

Third place match

Germany 3	**Austria 2**
Lehner (2), Conen	Seszta (2)

Final

Italy 2	**Czechoslovakia 1**
(after extra time)	
Combi (capt.), Monzeglio, Allemandi; Ferraris IV, Monti, Bertolini; Guaita, Meazza, Schiavio, Ferrari, Orsi.	Planicka (capt.); Zenisek, Ctyroky; Kostalek, Cambal, Krcil; Junek, Svoboda, Sobotka, Nejedly, Puc.

FRANCE 1938

Jules Rimet was the guiding light as far as the founding
of the World Cup was concerned, and it was in his
honour that the 1938 tournament was held in his home
country of France. Argentina refused to take part, upset
at not being chosen as hosts, completely disregarding
the wishes of the soccer-mad Argentinian people. The
third World Cup was played as the war clouds gathered
over Europe; the Spanish team was unable to compete
as the country was in a state of civil war.

There were thirty-six entries, but because Austria was
occupied by the Germans at the time, their team did not
compete. Germany took advantage of this by sprinkling
their own side with the pick of the Austrians who were,
at that time, one of the strongest international sides.
Although still not a member of FIFA, Britain was invited
to take part, but declined.

This was the first time that both holders and host
country were exempted until the final round. As in
1934, the tournament was played on a 'sudden-death'
knock-out basis, the fifteen participants being Sweden,
Belgium, Czechoslovakia, France, Germany, Holland,
Hungary, Italy, Norway, Poland, Romania and Switzerland from Europe, South America's only representative,
Brazil, with Cuba and the Dutch East Indies, like the
Poles, making their first appearance in the competition.

Aside from the strong German outfit, the most fancied
teams were: the Czechs, runners-up in 1934 and still
with Planicka in goal, the classic Nejedly at inside left
and Kostalek at right half; Italy, who had rebuilt

completely following their victory four years earlier; the Brazilians, who were confident but unpredictable; Sweden, who had been nicknamed the 'team of steel'; and Hungary, who had an abundance of World Cup experience and a high level of individual skill.

The surprise team was Cuba, who gave a fine display, beating Romania 2–1 in a replay. However, the Cubans came down to earth in the quarter-finals, being trounced 8–0 by Sweden, for whom Wetterstroem scored four. The most exciting game was on a mud-heap in Strasbourg, where Brazil and Poland had an eleven-goal thriller which Brazil won by the odd goal after extra time. The Brazilians showed for the first time their great potential, which we have come to appreciate and enjoy in every World Cup tournament since then. The host country was eliminated in the quarter-finals by the holders, Italy.

The tournament was marred somewhat by a disgracefully violent game between the Czechs and Brazil which ended in a 1–1 draw with only seventeen players on the field. Two Czechs finished up in hospital, one with a broken leg and the other with a broken arm. The replay was won 2–1 by Brazil, who made nine changes while the Czechs made six. Fortunately, that game was played without any incident of note.

The Final was between the holders, Italy, who had beaten Brazil 2–1 in the semi-final, and Hungary, 5–1 winners over Sweden after being one down after only thirty-five seconds. The Brazilians had paid the penalty for leaving out of the semi-final their star player Leonidas, nicknamed the 'black diamond', to keep him fresh for the Final. But the Final was well contested: the Italians were so disciplined and experienced that they wore down the skilful Hungarians and eventually won 4–2, which meant that in four triumphant years they had won two World Cups and an Olympic Gold. Piola, who scored two of the winners, was declared the outstanding player of this tournament.

The Second World War began just over twelve months later and there was a long gap of twelve years, until 1950, before the next tournament took place.

┌─── *AMAZING FACT* ─────────────────────────┐

The first goal scored in the World Cup was credited to Luis Laurent, for France against Mexico on 14 July 1930 in Montevideo, Uruguay. France won 4–1.

└──┘

Results

First round

Switzerland 1, Germany 1   Hungary 6, Dutch E. Indies 0
Switzerland 4, Germany 2   France 3, Belgium 1
(replay)   Czechoslovakia 3, Holland 0
Cuba 3, Romania 3   Brazil 6, Poland 5
Cuba 2, Romania 1   Italy 2, Norway 1
(replay)

Second round

Sweden 8, Cuba 0   Brazil 1, Czechoslovakia 1
Hungary 2, Switzerland 0   Brazil 2, Czechoslovakia 1
Italy 3, France 1   (replay)

Semi-finals

Italy 2   **Brazil 1**
Colaussi, Meazza (penalty)   Romeo

Hungary 5   **Sweden 1**
Szengeller (3), Titkos, Sarosi   Nyberg

Third place match

Brazil 4   **Sweden 2**
Romeo, Leonidas (2), Peracio   Jonasson, Nyberg

Final

Italy 4   **Hungary 2**
Olivieri; Foni, Rava;   Szabo; Polgar, Biro; Szalay,
Serantoni, Andreolo,   Szucs, Lazar; Sas, Vincze,

Locatelli; Biavati, Meazza (capt.), Piola, Ferrari, Colaussi.

Sarosi (capt.), Szengeller, Titkos.

BRAZIL 1950

In 1950 the tournament was held for the second time in South America, this time in Brazil, from whose team we were going to learn so much from this and subsequent World Cups. In fact, the Brazilians are nearly always one of the favourites to win and seldom disappoint their fanatical following, possessing skills the Europeans can rarely emulate.

Brazil's late entry into the Second World War had ensured that it was affected little by the hostilities, and its selection as a venue for the fourth World Cup fired the Brazilian people's enthusiasm even further. It was decided to build a new stadium at Maracana in Rio to house 200,000 spectators, but while it was used it was not fully completed when the tournament began.

As in Uruguay, the number of entrants was disappointingly low – only thirteen, which for the first time included England, the four British countries having rejoined FIFA in 1946. Scotland was also invited but declined to attend, having lost the home championship to England 1–0 at Hampden Park. The other surprising absentee was Argentina, who had some disagreement with the football authorities in Brazil and also decided to stay at home. Germany was still excluded from FIFA as a result of the war. The teams were divided into four groups, as follows:

Pool 1
Brazil, Mexico, Switzerland and Yugoslavia

Pool 2
Chile, England, Spain and USA

Pool 3
Italy, Paraguay and Sweden

Pool 4
Bolivia and Uruguay

Each group winner went on to the final stages, which were also played on a league basis. Two late withdrawals, France and India, had created uneven groups. Extraordinarily, there was not even a final game, although the last tie of the competition provided a superb 'final' in all but name. The organisation greatly favoured Brazil, who played five of their six games in Rio, whereas the other entries were forced to travel thousands of miles to stage their games in various parts of the country.

Italy, the holders of the Cup, competed even though the disaster of the Superga air crash in May 1949 had largely destroyed their chances. An aeroplane carrying the brilliant Torino team, returning from a friendly in Lisbon, crashed into the wall of a hillside monastery. Every player was killed, including eight of the Italian national side. Despite these circumstances, there was talent in the team.

Sweden were well managed by a Yorkshireman named George Raynor, who devoted his time to coaching individual players and making the team into a powerful force. The England team was also among the favourites, containing such illustrious names as Wright, Ramsey, Finney, Mortenson, Mannion, Milburn and Matthews. Brazil's preparations were thorough, in that the team was kept together in a house outside Rio; married men were unable to see their wives, and bedtime was ten o'clock sharp, before which each player had to take a vitamin drink.

The competition opened at the unfinished Maracana stadium, with huge traffic jams, scaffolding and rubble everywhere. A twenty-one-gun salute welcomed the Brazilian team on to the pitch, and an ecstatic crowd saw them win a 4–0 victory over Mexico.

The second pool provided the biggest surprise of the tournament, when the fancied England team faced a side of no-hopers from the USA on a bumpy pitch in a ramshackle stadium at Belo Horizonte. Despite the fact that England saw fit to leave Stanley Matthews sitting on the sidelines, they still had a formidable line-up which included Alf Ramsey, their manager in 1966. But everything went wrong for England: they hit the posts and crossbar, missed umpteen open goals, and then the inevitable happened – a cross, a touch with the head by Gaetjens, and England were well on the way to a defeat. Rather than being roused by adversity at least to get back on equal terms, things went from bad to worse and England lost ignominiously. To rub salt into open wounds, it was discovered that the Americans had had a night on the town the previous evening – they, too, had fully expected an English victory.

Football is full of surprises, and this was one of the biggest. England now had to beat Spain to get into the final group. They gave a much improved display, but what seemed to be a perfectly good goal by Jackie Milburn was disallowed, and they lost 1–0. Spain went through, and the other three finalists were Uruguay, Brazil and Sweden.

Brazil beat the Swedes 7–1 and the Spaniards by an emphatic five goals, 6–1. While they demonstrated skills in both games the like of which had not been seen before, in the game against Spain they played their now well-known art of possession football, and no doubt would have scored more if they had not decided to turn the game into an exhibition of their individual skills.

The final match saw them pitched against the well-disciplined and hard-tackling Uruguayan side. In the first half Brazil displayed their skills with non-stop attacking, but floundered against a brick-wall defence. Brazil pierced the barrier to take the lead in the second half, but this only inspired Uruguay to prove that they could attack as well as defend, and mid-way through the half, they equalised. The Brazilians disintegrated, and about ten minutes from the end Ghiggia scored the vital goal in a fine game which Brazil had only needed to draw to take the trophy. The excitement was such that three people died in the course of the match, and three more in the rejoicing afterwards.

Overall, the tournament was a great success. The official attendance at the final was 199,854, the highest ever attracted, and the average for each game was 60,772, a record which still stands. The twenty-two games were watched altogether by 1.34 million fans.

┌─ *AMAZING FACT* ─────────────────────────────────┐

Pelé of Brazil is the only player to have played with three
World Cup-winning teams, though he missed the 1962
Final because of injury. He made four appearances in
1958, two in 1962, six in 1970; he also appeared in two
games in 1966, for a total of fourteen appearances. Pelé
is the third-highest goal-scorer in World Cup Final
tournaments, with 12 goals.

└──┘

Results

First pool matches
Pool 1

Brazil 4, Mexico 0			Brazil 2, Switzerland 2		
Yugoslavia 3, Switzerland 0			Brazil 2, Yugoslavia 0		
Yugoslavia 4, Mexico 1			Switzerland 2, Mexico 1		

	P	W	D	L	F	A	Pts
Brazil	3	2	1	0	8	2	5
Yugoslavia	3	2	0	1	7	3	4
Switzerland	3	1	1	1	4	6	3
Mexico	3	0	0	3	2	10	0

Pool 2

Spain 3, United States 1		Spain 2, Chile 0	
England 2, Chile 0		Spain 1, England 0	
United States 1, England 0		Chile 5, United States 2	

	P	W	D	L	F	A	Pts
Spain	3	3	0	0	6	1	6
England	3	1	0	2	2	2	2
Chile	3	1	0	2	5	6	2
United States	3	1	0	2	4	8	2

Pool 3

Sweden 3, Italy 2		Italy 2, Paraguay 0
Sweden 2, Paraguay 2		

	P	W	D	L	F	A	Pts
Sweden	2	1	1	0	5	4	3
Italy	2	1	0	1	4	3	2
Paraguay	2	0	1	1	2	4	1

Pool 4
Uruguay 8, Bolivia 0

	P	W	D	L	F	A	Pts
Uruguay	1	1	0	0	8	0	2
Bolivia	1	0	0	1	0	8	0

Final pool matches
Uruguay 2   Spain 2
Brazil 7   Sweden 1
Uruguay 3   Sweden 2
Brazil 6   Spain 1
Sweden 3   Spain 1
Uruguay 2   Brazil 1

Final positions

	P	W	D	L	F	A	Pts
Uruguay	3	2	1	0	7	5	5
Brazil	3	2	0	1	14	4	4
Sweden	3	1	0	2	6	11	2
Spain	3	0	1	2	4	11	1

SWITZERLAND 1954

In 1954 this small host country was almost bursting at the seams with visitors who had come to see a tournament involving at least six teams with a high level of skill. Switzerland had been a strange choice for the staging of the fifth World Cup, and although it was accessible geographically, the organisation of the competition left a lot to be desired. A number of Eastern Bloc countries were now permitted entry. Germany, now divided into East and West, was establishing a pattern for the future and morale was being rebuilt. Once again the British home championship doubled as a qualifying group, and this time Scotland agreed to participate in the Finals.

The sixteen participants, sieved by a qualifying tournament, were each obliged to play only two first-round matches although they were divided into four pools of four. The arbitrary seeding of two countries in each group, to prevent their meeting in the first round, had a significant effect on the destiny of the Cup. The two seeded teams in each pool played only the two unseeded teams. The seeds in this case were Brazil, France, Hungary, Turkey, Uruguay, Austria, England and Italy, and they were pooled as follows:

Pool 1
Brazil, France, Mexico and Yugoslavia

Pool 2
Hungary, Turkey, South Korea and West Germany

Pool 3
Austria, Czechoslovakia, Scotland and Uruguay

Pool 4
Belgium, England, Italy and Switzerland

Another strange feature in a league-type competition was a decision to play extra time if the teams were drawn after ninety minutes. The top two teams in each pool progressed straight through to the quarter-finals, and from that point onwards the competition was played on a knock-out basis.

It was no surprise that Hungary, the 1952 Olympic champions, were favourites to win the fifth World Cup. Their attacking skills were tremendous, with Kocsis, Hidegkuti and Puskas always to the fore and backed up by some highly talented players. (In fact, Hungary were the first foreign side to beat England in the UK, with a magical display in November 1963 when they won 6–3, followed by a 7–1 victory in the return match in Budapest.)

West Germany were not much fancied from the start,

despite their admirable players Fritz, Otmar Walter and Horsteckel. Uruguay, the Cup holders, had another strong team and a couple of splendid wingers in Abbadie and Borges. Austria were marginally past their best, having boasted the best team in Europe three years earlier.

The tournament was not without incident, and the quarter-final between Hungary and Brazil has been referred to ever since as the 'Battle of Berne'. The match promised to be a football treat, but became a disaster. The Hungarians scored twice in the first ten minutes, but the game deteriorated, with players content to kick anything above grass regardless of whether it was ball or player. Brazil scored from a penalty, then Hungary reciprocated from a hotly disputed penalty kick. Brazil then scored a magnificent second. One player from each side was then sent off, followed shortly afterwards by a second Brazilian. The Hungarians scored another goal, and so won an apology of a game 4–2. Fighting on the pitch carried on in the dressing room, with fists and boots flying and police being called in to calm the proceedings.

The first semi-final saw Hungary beat Uruguay 4–2 after extra time in a splendid game between two great sides. This was the Uruguayans' first defeat in a World Cup match but it was probably their finest performance, and both teams were cheered from the pitch. The other semi-final, West Germany against Austria, was won by the Germans 6–1 thanks to a dreadful display by the Austrian goalkeeper.

The Final, between Hungary and West Germany, was expected to be a mere formality as the Hungarians had won a group match 8–1 against the Germans, who had clearly fielded a deliberately weakened side. After eight minutes Hungary were two up, but the Germans scored twice shortly afterwards. Hungary then hit the post and also the crossbar. The West German goalkeeper put on a heroic performance, and with both sides playing brilliantly it took a tragic error in the Hungarian defence to allow Germany in for the winner. A significant factor in their defeat had been in persisting with injured Puskas, who became a real burden as he played bravely on. After a formidable run of victories, the 'Magical Magyars' had at last been defeated. West Germany had pulled off a remarkable comeback to crown an exceptional World Cup competition.

Results

Pool 1

Yugoslavia 1, France 0   France 3, Mexico 2
Brazil 5, Mexico 0   Brazil 1, Yugoslavia 1

	P	W	D	L	F	A	Pts
Brazil	2	1	1	0	6	1	3
Yugoslavia	2	1	1	0	2	1	3
France	2	1	0	1	3	3	2
Mexico	2	0	0	2	2	8	0

Pool 2

Hungary 9, Korea 0   Hungary 8, W. Germany 3
W. Germany 4, Turkey 1   Turkey 7, Korea 0

	P	W	D	L	F	A	Pts
Hungary	2	2	0	0	17	3	4
W. Germany	2	1	0	1	7	9	2
Turkey	2	1	0	1	8	4	2
Korea	2	0	0	2	0	16	0

Play-off W. Germany 7, Turkey 2

Pool 3

Austria 1, Scotland 0   Austria 5, Czechoslovakia 0
Uruguay 2, Czechoslovakia 0   Uruguay 7, Scotland 0

	P	W	D	L	F	A	Pts
Uruguay	2	2	0	0	9	0	4
Austria	2	2	0	0	6	0	4
Czechoslovakia	2	0	0	2	0	7	0
Scotland	2	0	0	2	0	8	0

Pool 4
England 4, Belgium 4   Switzerland 2, Italy 1
England 2, Switzerland 0   Italy 4, Belgium 1

	P	W	D	L	F	A	Pts
England	2	1	1	0	6	4	3
Italy	2	1	0	1	5	3	2
Switzerland	2	1	0	1	2	3	2
Belgium	2	0	1	1	5	8	1

Play-off Switzerland 4, Italy 1

Quarter-finals
W. Germany 2   Yugoslavia 0
Hungary 4   Brazil 2
Austria 7   Switzerland 5
Uruguay 4   England 2

Semi-finals
W. Germany 6   **Austria 1**
Schaefer, Morlock, Walter, F.   Probst
(2 penalties), Walter, O. (2)

Hungary 4   **Uruguay 2**
Czibor, Hidegkuti, Kocsis (2)   Hohberg (2)

Third place match
Austria 3   **Uruguay 1**
Stojaspal (penalty), Cruz   Hohberg
(own goal), Ocwirk

Final
W. Germany 3   **Hungary 2**
Turek; Posipal, Kohlmeyer;   Grosics; Buzansky, Lantos;
Eckel, Liebrich, Mai; Rahn,   Bozsik, Lorant, Zakarias;
Morlock, Walter, O., Walter,   Czibor, Kocsis, Hidegkuti,
F., Schaefer.   Puskas, Toth, J.

SCORERS   SCORERS
Morlock, Rahn (2)   Puskas, Czibor
(HT 2/2)

SWEDEN 1958

For the first time, the 1958 Finals were staged in Scandinavia, with Sweden the venue. It was also the first time that all four British countries qualified for the final stage, although Wales made it only because of a late withdrawal. Sweden had won the Olympic soccer title in 1948, with a team of outstanding players.

The original entries numbered fifty-three, the highest so far. There were some surprises among the teams who failed to qualify, for example Uruguay – ousted by virtual unknowns Paraguay – Italy, Spain and Switzerland. The countries which progressed to the Finals were grouped into pools of four as in 1954, but this time the seeding arrangement was dropped, and each country played three games. Once again, the top two teams in each group progressed to the quarter-finals which were played on the basis of a sudden-death knock-out, as were the later rounds. In the event of two countries tying for second place on points, goal difference was disregarded and play-offs were used as a decider. The countries were pooled as follows:

Pool 1
Argentina, Czechoslovakia, Northern Ireland and West Germany

Pool 2
France, Paraguay, Scotland and Yugoslavia

Pool 3
Hungary, Mexico, Sweden and Wales

Pool 4
Austria, Brazil, England and Russia

While few were prepared to state their fancies as

winners, Brazil with Didì and Garrincha must have been high on anyone's list. The England team had been depleted a few months earlier when, in early February, the tragic Munich air crash deprived the side of three regular players in the young giant Duncan Edwards, Tommy Taylor and Roger Byrne. Edwards could undoubtedly have become one of the all-time greats and worn the England shirt for many years, as he was still in his teens when the tragedy occurred.

The Swedish press and public had no confidence in their own team's chances, but as the Swedes made progress, the home crowd got right behind them. Since their victory in Berne, little had gone right for the West Germans and no fewer than seven of the 1954 team had fallen by the wayside.

In the play-offs for the group qualifying games, Wales did well to overcome the Hungarians 2–1, with goals from Ivor Allchurch and Terry Medwin, while Northern Ireland beat the Czechs 2–1. However, the hopes of having three home countries in the quarter-finals were dashed when England were beaten 1–0 by Russia.

The quarter-finals saw Germany beat Yugoslavia 1–0. Sweden beat Russia 2–0, and France beat Northern Ireland 4–0. Wales gave probably one of their best performances, despite the absence of John Charles. They defended like tigers to thwart the brilliant tactics of Brazil, and only a lucky goal by seventeen-year-old Pelé separated the teams at the end.

In the first semi-final the hosts, Sweden, beat West Germany 2–1 in a bad-tempered match, poorly controlled by a Hungarian referee who sent off a German player in the second half. The other semi-final was played between the now favourites Brazil, who had yet to concede a goal, and France, the sensation of the tournament with their goal-scoring achievements and who at least had the satisfaction of scoring twice. However, Brazil hit five, three of them put into the net by their fabulous rising star Pelé. France redeemed themselves somewhat in the third-place play-off by beating Germany 6–3, with Fontaine scoring four to bring his total for the Finals to thirteen, a record which still stands today.

The Final took place in Stockholm, the 'Venice of the North'. The atmosphere was electric with Sweden, the home country, playing against the brilliant, unpredictable Brazilians. George Raynor, Sweden's British manager, predicted that an early Swedish goal would throw Brazil into panic, but after Liedholm had put Sweden ahead in the fourth minute, he was soon forced to eat his words. Within six minutes Vavà had equalised and then Brazil really turned on the magic, with Pelé thundering a shot against the Swedes' post. Vavà scored a second goal in the thirty-second minute and then, ten minutes into the second half, Pelé scored one of the greatest goals ever seen in a World Cup Final when he took a high ball on his thigh, hooked it over his head and, spinning round, volleyed it into the Swedish goal. The Swedes were now demoralised and went down to 4–1 in the final quarter of an hour, to a goal by Zagalo. Sweden pulled back a goal through Simonsson, but then Pelé found Zagalo with a centre to bring their final total up to five. The World Cup was Brazil's at long last, and they ran like excited children around the pitch, holding first their own flag and then the Swedes'. The best team in the competition had won the title.

Results

Pool 1
W. Germany 2, Czechoslovakia 2 Argentina 3, N. Ireland 1
N. Ireland 1, Czechoslovakia 0 W. Germany 2, N. Ireland 2
W. Germany 3, Argentina 1   Czechoslovakia 6, Argentina 1

	P	W	D	L	F	A	Pts
W. Germany	3	1	2	0	7	5	4
Czechoslovakia	3	1	1	1	8	4	3
N. Ireland	3	1	1	1	4	5	3
Argentina	3	1	0	2	5	10	2

Play-off N. Ireland 2, Czechoslovakia 1

Pool 2

France 7, Paraguay 3   Paraguay 3, Scotland 2
Yugoslavia 1, Scotland 1   France 2, Scotland 1
Yugoslavia 3, France 2   Yugoslavia 3, Paraguay 3

	P	W	D	L	F	A	Pts
France	3	2	0	1	11	7	4
Yugoslavia	3	1	2	0	7	6	4
Paraguay	3	1	1	1	9	12	3
Scotland	3	0	1	2	4	6	1

Pool 3

Sweden 3, Mexico 0   Sweden 2, Hungary 1
Hungary 1, Wales 1   Sweden 0, Wales 0
Wales 1, Mexico 1   Hungary 4, Mexico 0

	P	W	D	L	F	A	Pts
Sweden	3	2	1	0	5	1	5
Hungary	3	1	1	1	6	3	3
Wales	3	0	3	0	2	2	3
Mexico	3	0	1	2	1	8	1

Play-off Wales 2, Hungary 1

Pool 4

England 2, Russia 2   Russia 2, Austria 0
Brazil 3, Austria 0   Brazil 2, Russia 0
England 0, Brazil 0   England 2, Austria 2

	P	W	D	L	F	A	Pts
Brazil	3	2	1	0	5	0	5
England	3	0	3	0	4	4	3
Russia	3	1	1	1	4	4	3
Austria	3	0	1	2	2	7	1

Play-off Russia 1, England 0

Quarter-finals

France 4   N. Ireland 0
West Germany 1   Yugoslavia 0

31

| Sweden 2 | Russia 0 |
| Brazil 1 | Wales 0 |

Semi-finals

| Brazil 5 | France 2 |
| Vavà, Didì, Pelé (3) | Fontaine, Piantoni |

| Sweden 3 | West Germany 1 |
| Skoglund, Gren, Hamrin | Schaefer |

Third place match

France 6	West Germany 3
Fontaine (4), Kopa (penalty),	Cieslarezyk, Rahn, Schaefer
Douis	

Final

Brazil 5	Sweden 2
Gilmar; Santos, D., Santos,	Svensson; Bergmark,
N.; Zito, Bellini, Orlando;	Axbom; Boerjesson,
Garrincha, Didì, Vavà, Pelé,	Gustavsson, Parling;
Zagalo.	Hamrin, Gren, Simonsson,
	Liedholm, Skoglund.

SCORERS	SCORERS
Vavà (2), Pelé (2), Zagalo	Liedholm, Simonsson
(HT 2/1)	

CHILE 1962

Many people thought that Chile was chosen to stage the seventh World Cup as an act of sympathy, the President of that country's FA having pleaded: 'We must have the World Cup because we have nothing else.' This long, narrow strip of a country up the western side of South America had recently been devastated by severe earthquakes. However, FIFA must have been impressed by the Chileans' determination, and realising that after two successive European finals a South American venue should be chosen, agreed to Chile's request. The Chileans quickly started building a superb new stadium in the capital, Santiago, and another at Vinadelmar, to help compensate for the poorer stadia elsewhere.

The format was the same as in 1958, with four groups (no longer called 'pools') of four countries, each playing one another and the top two of each group progressing to the quarter-finals. Unlike all previous competitions, in the event of a tie, with two countries scoring the same number of points, goal difference was to be used to determine the qualifiers. The countries were grouped as follows:

Group 1
Columbia, Uruguay, Russia and Yugoslavia

Group 2
Chile, Italy, Switzerland and West Germany

Group 3
Brazil, Czechoslovakia, Mexico and Spain

Group 4
Argentina, Bulgaria, England and Hungary

The favourites were the current champions, Brazil. They had lost several of their star players, including Vavà and Didì, to European football, but they returned prior to the competition. Garrincha, the 'little bird', was still there, crippled since childhood but a footballer of superb natural gifts, astounding speed and swerve. There were changes in the central defence, however, with Mauro taking over at centre-half from Bellini. The Czechs were known to be a gifted team though a slow one – slowness meant precision, and there were some excellent ball-players in the team. England were the only UK representatives, and had Walter Winterbottom in charge of his fourth and last World Cup campaign. The England attack was still built around Fulham's inside-left Johnny Haynes, but there were exciting newcomers in the prolific goal-scorer Jimmy Greaves and the calm, stylish half-back Bobby Moore. Chile were seen as an outside chance; they were bound to be spurred on by their own supporters, and had lately thrashed Hungary.

The tournament itself was rather insignificant, with no high-scoring games as on previous occasions. There was a blood-and-thunder game between Russia and Yugoslavia, although surprisingly there was nobody sent off despite one player even aiming a blow at the referee. The Yugoslavs were involved in another game of high drama against Uruguay when a player from each side was sent off.

The game in which feelings ran highest was Chile against Italy, principally because an Italian journalist had written an article into which he poured all manner of criticisms upon Chile in general, and the people in particular. The Italians' habit of taking South American players of Italian extraction to strengthen their own team did nothing to keep tempers down. In only the seventh minute, Italy's Ferrini was sent off after kicking Landa but refused to leave the pitch until eight minutes later, when he was escorted off by police. A second Italian got his marching orders on the stroke of half-time for kicking an opponent; the Chilean player had his nose broken. All in all the game, which Chile won 2–0, was a disgrace to the name of football, thoroughly meriting its nickname of the 'Battle of Santiago'.

In the quarter-finals England were drawn against probably the only opponents they did not want – Brazil – and not surprisingly lost 3–1. Even so, they were not disgraced. The Chileans won their quarter-final against Russia, their progress in the tournament probably being as much of a surprise to them as it was to everyone else. Czechoslovakia beat Hungary, and Yugoslavia beat Germany.

The most emotional of the semi-finals was Chile against Brazil, which had some fine moments of football and also featured some best-forgotten scenes. Garrincha gave Brazil a two-goal lead but was sent off with Landa and had his head cut by a flying bottle. The Brazilians missed the class of Pelé, injured in an earlier match, but nevertheless kept a grip on the game in spite of some rough treatment. Brazil eventually won 4–2, to reach their second successive Final. In the other semi-final, Czechoslovakia silenced their critics by beating the talented Yugoslavs 3–1.

The Final was not a great match. Brazil were the favourites, but the Czechs had made many people sit up and take notice. Czechoslovakia initially took the lead, but Brazil equalised before half-time and then scored two more in the last twenty minutes, to become the first team for twenty-four years to win successive tournaments.

Results

Group 1

Uruguay 2, Colombia 1   Russia 4, Colombia 4
Russia 2, Yugoslavia 0   Russia 2, Uruguay 1
Yugoslavia 3, Uruguay 1   Yugoslavia 5, Colombia 0

	P	W	D	L	F	A	Pts
Russia	3	2	1	0	8	5	5
Yugoslavia	3	2	0	1	8	3	4
Uruguay	3	1	0	2	4	6	2
Colombia	3	0	1	2	5	11	1

Group 2

Chile 3, Switzerland 1   Germany 2, Switzerland 1
Germany 0, Italy 0   Germany 2, Chile 0
Chile 2, Italy 0   Italy 3, Switzerland 0

	P	W	D	L	F	A	Pts
Germany	3	2	1	0	4	1	5
Chile	3	2	0	1	5	3	4
Italy	3	1	1	1	3	2	3
Switzerland	3	0	0	3	2	8	0

Group 3

Brazil 2, Mexico 0
Czechoslovakia 1, Spain 0
Brazil 0, Czechoslovakia 0

Spain 1, Mexico 0
Brazil 2, Spain 1
Mexico 3, Czechoslovakia 1

	P	W	D	L	F	A	Pts
Brazil	3	2	1	0	4	1	5
Czechoslovakia	3	1	1	1	2	3	3
Mexico	3	1	0	2	3	4	2
Spain	3	1	0	2	2	3	2

Group 4

Argentina 1, Bulgaria 0
Hungary 2, England 1
England 3, Argentina 1

Hungary 6, Bulgaria 1
Argentina 0, Hungary 0
England 0, Bulgaria 0

	P	W	D	L	F	A	Pts
Hungary	3	2	1	0	8	2	5
England	3	1	1	1	4	3	3
Argentina	3	1	1	1	2	3	3
Bulgaria	3	0	1	2	1	7	1

Quarter-finals

Yugoslavia 1   **West Germany 0**
Brazil 3   **England 1**
Chile 2   **Russia 1**
Czechoslovakia 1   **Hungary 0**

Semi-finals

Brazil 4
Garrincha (2), Vavà (2)

Chile 2
Toro, Sanchez, L. (penalty)

Czechoslovakia 3
Kadraba, Scherer (2)

Yugoslavia 1
Jerkovic

Third place match

Chile 1
Rojas

Yugoslavia 0

Final

Brazil 3
Gilmar; Santos, D., Mauro,
Zozimo, Santos, N.; Zito,
Didì; Garrincha, Vavà,
Amarildo, Zagalo.
SCORERS
Amarildo, Zito, Vavà
(HT 1/1)

Czechoslovakia 1
Schroiff; Tichy, Novak;
Pluskal, Popluhar, Masopust,
Pospichal, Scherer, Kvasniak,
Kadraba, Jelinek.
SCORER
Masopust

ENGLAND 1966

It was a pity that, for the second successive tournament, England as host nation was the only country from the British Isles to qualify for the Finals. The sixteen qualifiers looked good for an interesting competition, which was played in exactly the same format as in the 1962 series. The participants were grouped as follows:

Group 1
(Wembley and White City)
England, France, Mexico and Uruguay

Group 2
(Villa Park and Hillsborough)
Argentina, Spain, Switzerland and West Germany

Group 3
(Goodison Park and Old Trafford)
Brazil, Bulgaria, Hungary and Portugal

Group 4
(Ayresome Park and Roker Park)
Chile, Italy, North Korea and Russia

England was managed by former international Alf Ramsey, who had achieved success with Ipswich in the Football League, taking them from the Third Division to champions of the First in successive seasons. He had accepted the job on condition that he alone picked the team rather than, as hitherto, in conjunction with a selection committee. Ramsey soon transformed Bobby Charlton into the general of the team; Martin Peters blossomed in his new midfield role; and in selecting Gordon Banks as goalkeeper and Jack Charlton to play alongside Bobby Moore at the back, the defence had been strengthened considerably.

Brazil had stayed faithful to their old guard, and at

twenty-five Pelé was at the peak of his career. In Eusebio, Portugal had one of the game's great stars, an inside-forward with strength, acceleration and a devastating right foot. The West Germans were playing things close to their chest, but in midfield there was an abundance of young talent – Wolfgang Overath, Helmut Haller, and an elegant attacking half named Franz Beckenbauer, from Bayern Munich.

Alas, particularly at Wembley, the football prior to the semi-finals was dull and uninteresting. There were some good games with fine football in the other centres, however. The team that captured the hearts of the north-eastern crowds were the little North Koreans, beaten 3–0 by Russia in the first match but by learning and improving their play, astounding everyone by eliminating the Italians 1–0 to qualify for the quarter-finals. After having won two of the three World Cup tournaments before the war, this defeat stunned the Italians who headed for home with their dismal post-war record in the competition unredeemed.

The Koreans then journeyed across the Pennines to Goodison Park to meet Portugal, who had a useful team including the crowd-pulling Eusebio. The Koreans scored early on, and soon added two more to lead 3–0. They were waltzing around the Portuguese at will, but Eusebio decided enough was enough and pulled two back before half-time. He scored two more before Augusto added a fifth, which saw them into the semi-final, but not before they had had the fright of their lives.

The other quarter-final games, surprisingly, did not include Brazil. England met Argentina in an eventful game. The Argentinian captain, Rattin, was sent off but refused to go. It was about ten minutes before he left and the match could be restarted. Fortunately, Hurst scored in the second half of an ill-tempered game, to give England a semi-final place despite a poor display.

The semi-finals paired England and Portugal, a match which England won 2–1, with much heart-pounding towards the end. When the Portuguese, inspired by Eusebio, turned on the pressure to try for the equaliser, their efforts were thwarted by Gordon Banks, who was in great form. West Germany beat Russia 2–1 to gain the other place in the Final.

There was an electric atmosphere in Wembley for the Final, in which Germany initially took the lead. Ray Wilson uncharacteristically headed Held's left-wing cross straight to the feet of Haller on the far post. Haller controlled the ball cleanly and drove it low and wide across Banks into the left-hand corner. England equalised a few minutes later, through Hurst. Peters gave England the lead in the second half, but with the crowd cheering for an England victory, a free kick saw Weber equalise with about ninety seconds to go. During the interval before extra time, Alf Ramsey marched on to the field and told his players that they had won the World Cup once and now they must win it again.

Hurst scored twice during this extra period, and the first of these goals will for ever be a controversial topic,

because there was much disagreement as to whether or not the ball crossed the line. Hurst had thundered the shot which hit the underside of the bar and bounced down, leaving Tilkowski with no chance. Roger Hunt stood with his arms joyfully raised, not bothering to give a final touch as he clearly thought the ball had crossed the line. Whether or not it had, the goal counted and Hurst had the only hat-trick scored in a World Cup Final.

So the eighth World Cup had a fairy-tale finale. Interest in football in Britain was rekindled, albeit temporarily, as a result of England's victory, and a new band of spectators began to fill the grounds. Television coverage had been immense and it was estimated that 400 million people throughout the world had seen the Final, a game rich in entertainment value. The total attendance figure for the thirty-two matches was almost 1.65 million, giving an average of almost 51,000 per match. The England manager, Alf Ramsey, was later knighted in recognition of this famous victory.

── *AMAZING FACT* ─────────────────

Gordon Banks conceded only 3 goals in England's 6 matches during the 1966 Finals.

Results

Group 1

England 0, Uruguay 0	England 2, Mexico 0
France 1, Mexico 1	Uruguay 0, Mexico 0
Uruguay 2, France 1	England 2, France 0

	P	W	D	L	F	A	Pts
England	3	2	1	0	4	0	5
Uruguay	3	1	2	0	2	1	4
Mexico	3	0	2	1	1	3	2
France	3	0	1	2	2	5	1

Group 2

W. Germany 5, Switzerland 0   Argentina 0, W. Germany 0
Argentina 2, Spain 1   Argentina 2, Switzerland 0
Spain 2, Switzerland 1   West Germany 2, Spain 1

	P	W	D	L	F	A	Pts
West Germany	3	2	1	0	7	1	5
Argentina	3	2	1	0	4	1	5
Spain	3	1	0	2	4	5	2
Switzerland	3	0	0	3	1	9	0

Group 3

Brazil 2, Bulgaria 0   Portugal 3, Bulgaria 0
Portugal 3, Hungary 1   Portugal 3, Brazil 1
Hungary 3, Brazil 1   Hungary 3, Bulgaria 1

	P	W	D	L	F	A	Pts
Portugal	3	3	0	0	9	2	6
Hungary	3	2	0	1	7	5	4
Brazil	3	1	0	2	4	6	2
Bulgaria	3	0	0	3	1	8	0

Group 4

Russia 3, North Korea 0   Russia 1, Italy 0
Italy 2, Chile 0   North Korea 1, Italy 0
Chile 1, North Korea 1   Russia 2, Chile 1

	P	W	D	L	F	A	Pts
Russia	3	3	0	0	6	1	6
North Korea	3	1	1	1	2	4	3
Italy	3	1	0	2	2	2	2
Chile	3	0	1	2	2	5	1

Quarter-finals

England 1   **Argentina 0**
West Germany 4 **Uruguay 0**
Portugal 5   **North Korea 3**
Russia 2   **Hungary 1**

Semi-finals

West Germany 2   **Russia 1**
Haller, Beckenbauer   Porkujan

England 2   **Portugal 1**
Charlton, R. (2)   Eusebio (penalty)

Third place match
Portugal 2
Eusebio (penalty), Torres

Russia 1
Malafeev

Final
England 4
(after extra time)
Banks; Cohen, Wilson; Stiles,
Charlton, J., Moore; Ball,
Hurst, Hunt, Charlton, R.,
Peters.

West Germany 2

Tilkowski; Hottges, Schulz,
Weber, Schnellinger; Haller,
Beckenbauer, Overath;
Seeler, Held, Emmerich.

SCORERS
Hurst (3), Peters
(HT 1/1 FT 2/2)

SCORERS
Haller, Weber

MEXICO 1970

Another new location, Mexico, was chosen for the ninth
World Cup. It had been expected that the competition
would be staged in Argentina, but Mexico petitioned
and were selected for the series despite the disadvan-
tages of heat and altitude.

England was the only UK country that qualified, as
champions, to travel to Mexico. The system of geogra-
phical grouping meant that the stronger footballing
nations of western and eastern Europe were pitted
against one another. New to the final stages were El
Salvador, Israel and Morocco. The competition was
played in exactly the same format as the eighth World
Cup, with four groups of four leading straight to the
quarter-finals, but for the first time, substitutes were
allowed.

Group 1
(Mexico City)
Belgium, El Salvador, Mexico and Russia

Group 2
(Toluca and Puebla)
Israel, Italy, Sweden and Uruguay

Group 3
(Guadalajara)
Brazil, Czechoslovakia, England and Rumania

Group 4
(Leon)
Bulgaria, Morocco, Peru and West Germany

The decision to bring many of the games forward to noon for the benefit of the worldwide television audiences meant playing in temperatures approaching 100°F.

Brazil's preparations had been hampered by a change of management shortly before the Finals, with Saldanha replaced by Zagalo, their left-winger in the victories of 1958 and 1962. Zagalo made important changes, including using inside-forward Rivelino as a left-winger. England were hopeful of retaining the Cup but became the team the Mexicans loved to hate, a 'team of thieves and drunkards' as one local newspaper put it. The ridiculous accusation that Bobby Moore had stolen goods from a jewellery shop did not, however, affect his immaculate performances in the competition. For West Germany there was a new and formidable threat in the person of Gerd Muller, a striker with a deadly finish. Italy's hopes rested mainly with Riva's great goal-scoring talent.

There were few surprises in the opening rounds and the qualifiers for the quarter-finals were more or less as expected: Mexico *v* Italy, Russia *v* Uruguay, Brazil *v* Peru, and England *v* West Germany. The Mexico *v* Italy game got off to the start which the host nation's supporters had hoped for with the Mexicans taking the lead after twelve minutes, but Italy equalised before half-time and began really to play in the second half, scoring three more before the end. It was the first time the Italians had reached the semi-finals since 1938. Russia and Uruguay played out a bad-tempered game best forgotten. The tie was settled in the last minute of extra time, when Uruguay scored a hotly disputed goal. The best game was between Brazil and Peru, which the former won 4–2. The fourth game put West Germany into the semi-final when they beat England, deprived through illness of Gordon Banks, 3–2 after extra time after being two goals down. England had struggled after the substitution of Charlton and Peters by Bell and Hunter, and the Germans took full advantage, gaining revenge for their defeat in the Final four years earlier. England could only blame themselves for allowing West Germany back into the game. They had thus missed a chance to meet Italy in the semi-final in a game which the Italians won 4–3 after extra time. Throughout the match there was never more than one goal between the teams in a nail-biting encounter. Brazil had a fairly easy 3–1 victory against Uruguay in the other semi-final.

The Italians were probably as surprised as anyone at reaching the Final, and no one gave them a chance of winning the match. This proved prophetic, as they were beaten 4–1 in the Aztec Stadium by the Brazilian side, who gave another classy performance to win the Jules Rimet Trophy for the third time, a feat which enabled them to take it home to Rio as their own property. It was estimated that almost 800 million people world-wide had watched the match on television.

Results

Group 1

Mexico 0, Russia 0	Mexico 4, El Salvador 0
Belgium 3, El Salvador 0	Russia 2, El Salvador 0
Russia 4, Belgium 1	Mexico 1, Belgium 0

	P	W	D	L	F	A	Pts
Russia	3	2	1	0	6	1	5
Mexico	3	2	1	0	5	0	5
Belgium	3	1	0	2	4	5	2
El Salvador	3	0	0	3	0	9	0

Group 2

Uruguay 2, Israel 0	Sweden 1, Israel 1
Italy 1, Sweden 0	Sweden 1, Uruguay 0
Uruguay 0, Italy 0	Italy 0, Israel 0

	P	W	D	L	F	A	Pts
Italy	3	1	2	0	1	0	4
Uruguay	3	1	1	1	2	1	3
Sweden	3	1	1	1	2	2	3
Israel	3	0	2	1	1	3	2

Group 3

England 1, Romania 0	Brazil 1, England 0
Brazil 4, Czechoslovakia 1	Brazil 3, Romania 2
Romania 2, Czechoslovakia 1	England 1, Czechoslovakia 0

	P	W	D	L	F	A	Pts
Brazil	3	3	0	0	8	3	6
England	3	2	0	1	2	1	4
Romania	3	1	0	2	4	5	2
Czechoslovakia	3	0	0	3	2	7	0

Group 4

Peru 3, Bulgaria 2	West Germany 5, Bulgaria 2
West Germany 2, Morocco 1	West Germany 3, Peru 1
Peru 3, Morocco 0	Morocco 1, Bulgaria 1

	P	W	D	L	F	A	Pts
West Germany	3	3	0	0	10	4	6
Peru	3	2	0	1	7	5	4
Bulgaria	3	0	1	2	5	9	1
Morocco	3	0	1	2	2	6	1

Quarter-finals
West Germany 3   **England 2**
Brazil 4   **Peru 2**
Italy 4   **Mexico 1**
Uruguay 1   **Russia 0**

Semi-finals
Italy 4   **West Germany 3**
Boninsegna, Burgnich, Riva,   Schnellinger, Muller (2)
Rivera

Brazil 3   **Uruguay 1**
Clodoaldo, Jairzinho,   Cubilla
Rivelino

Third place match
West Germany 1   **Uruguay 0**
Overath

Final
Brazil 4   **Italy 1**
Felix; Carlos Alberto, Brito,   Albertosi; Cera; Burgnich,
Piazza, Everaldo; Clodoaldo,   Bertini (Juliano), Rosato,
Gerson; Jairzinho, Tostao,   Facchetti; Domenghini,
Pelé, Rivelino.   Mazzola, De Sisti;
Boninsegna (Rivera), Riva.

SCORERS   SCORER
Pelé, Gerson, Jairzinho,   Boninsegna
Carlos Alberto
(HT 1/1)

WEST GERMANY 1974

For this, the tenth World Cup competition, a completely
new trophy replaced the original, won outright by Brazil
in 1970. It was paid for by FIFA, who had turned down
Brazil's generous offer to provide the replacement.
Security for the series was very tight after the horrific
massacre of Israel's athletes at the 1972 Olympic Games
in West Germany.

For the first time since 1950, the idea of groups was

extended beyond the first-round games. The Final itself
was retained, but the semi-finals were entirely dispensed
with, the finalists and third-place play-off teams being
the winners and runners-up respectively of the two
second-stage groups. As before, sixteen nations competed and these were divided into four first-round
groups of four, the top two of which progressed to
second-round groups of four countries.

England failed to qualify for the Finals for the first
time since rejoining FIFA after the Second World War,
and Scotland were Britain's only representatives. West
Germany as hosts, and Brazil as champions, were
automatically included in the final sixteen teams. New
teams included East Germany, Australia (which became
the first Oceania country to reach the Finals) and Zaire
(the first Central African country to do so), while Haiti
made their first appearance representing Central and
North America. The countries were grouped as follows:

Group 1
Australia, Chile, East Germany and West Germany

Group 2
Brazil, Scotland, Yugoslavia and Zaire

Group 3
Bulgaria, Holland, Sweden and Uruguay

Group 4
Argentina, Haiti, Italy and Poland

The West Germans, like the Dutch, played total football, which meant that forwards could become defenders and vice versa. Beckenbauer played in the role of
attacking sweeper, moving upfield to maximum effect.
Holland had a host of talented players including Cruyff,
van Hanegen, Johann Neeskens, and the adventurous
veteran Jongbloed in goal. Poland's fine side had elimi-

nated England, a fact which eventually led to Alf Ramsey's dismissal. Brazil were to be blitzed by injuries to the brilliant Pelé, Tostao and Gerson, and in the end their defensive methods let them down.

The teams to catch the eye in the first round were Holland and Poland, who each won their respective groups, the latter with a 100 per cent victory record. The East Germans also came top in their group unbeaten, including a victory over West Germany, who finished second. The leaders in the fourth group were Yugoslavia, also unbeaten, their 9–0 score over Haiti being the highest score in these Finals.

Holland continued their great form and reached the Final undefeated in their league, which included a 2–0 victory over Brazil. West Germany won their three games to set the scene for a great Final between next-door neighbours.

English football was honoured by the selection of Jack Taylor of Wolverhampton to referee the Final. He was respected all over the world and nowhere more than in the English Football League. It did not take him long to make a mark on the Final. He awarded a penalty to Holland in the first two minutes, when Cruyff was fouled. Neeskens scored from the spot, only for Holzenbein to be fouled at the other end, and again from the spot Breitner equalised. Play continued to excite the home crowd and before half-time the German goal-scoring machine, Muller, put them in the lead, a position they hung on to despite desperate efforts by the Dutch, who were magnificent in defeat. It was generally agreed that it was a shame there had to be a losing team. Nevertheless, the hosts, West Germany, became the first holders of the new trophy.

Results

First pool matches
Group 1

West Germany 1, Chile 0   East Germany 1,
East Germany 2, Australia 0   West Germany 0
West Germany 3, Australia 0   Chile 0, Australia 0
East Germany 1, Chile 1

	P	W	D	L	F	A	Pts
East Germany	3	2	1	0	4	1	5
West Germany	3	2	0	1	4	1	4
Chile	3	0	2	1	1	2	1
Australia	3	0	1	2	0	5	1

Group 2

Brazil 0, Yugoslavia 0   Yugoslavia 9, Zaire 0
Scotland 2, Zaire 0   Scotland 1, Yugoslavia 1
Brazil 0, Scotland 0   Brazil 3, Zaire 0

	P	W	D	L	F	A	Pts
Yugoslavia	3	1	2	0	10	1	4
Brazil	3	1	2	0	3	0	4
Scotland	3	1	2	0	3	1	4
Zaire	3	0	0	3	0	14	0

Group 3

Holland 2, Uruguay 0   Bulgaria 1, Uruguay 1
Sweden 0, Bulgaria 0   Holland 4, Bulgaria 1
Holland 0, Sweden 0   Sweden 3, Uruguay 0

	P	W	D	L	F	A	Pts
Holland	3	2	1	0	6	1	5
Sweden	3	1	2	0	3	0	4
Bulgaria	3	0	2	1	2	5	2
Uruguay	3	0	1	2	1	6	1

Group 4

Italy 3, Haiti 1
Poland 3, Argentina 2
Italy 1, Argentina 1

Poland 7, Haiti 0
Argentina 4, Haiti 1
Poland 2, Italy 1

	P	W	D	L	F	A	Pts
Poland	3	3	0	0	12	3	6
Argentina	3	1	1	1	7	5	3
Italy	3	1	1	1	5	4	3
Haiti	3	0	0	3	2	14	0

Second pool matches
Group A

Brazil 1, East Germany 0
Holland 4, Argentina 0
Holland 2, East Germany 0

Brazil 2, Argentina 1
Holland 2, Brazil 0
Argentina 1, East Germany 1

	P	W	D	L	F	A	Pts
Holland	3	3	0	0	8	0	6
Brazil	3	2	0	1	3	3	4
East Germany	3	0	1	2	1	4	1
Argentina	3	0	1	2	2	7	1

Group B

Poland 1, Sweden 0
West Germany 2, Yugoslavia 0
Poland 2, Yugoslavia 1

West Germany 4, Sweden 2
Sweden 2, Yugoslavia 1
West Germany 1, Poland 0

	P	W	D	L	F	A	Pts
West Germany	3	3	0	0	7	2	6
Poland	3	2	0	1	3	2	4
Sweden	3	1	0	2	4	6	2
Yugoslavia	3	0	0	3	2	6	0

Third place match
Poland 1
Lato

Brazil 0

Final
West Germany 2
Maier; Beckenbauer; Vogts,
Schwarzenbeck, Breitner;
Bonhof, Hoeness, Overath;
Grabowski, Muller,
Holzenbein.

Holland 1
Jongbloed; Suurbier,
Rijsbergen (De Jong), Haan,
Krol; Jansen, Neeskens, van
Hanegen; Rep, Cruyff,
Rensenbrink (van de
Kerkhof, R.).

ARGENTINA 1978

The Finals once again went back to South America and, for the first time, to Argentina. There were misgivings in Europe owing to the military dictatorship established in Buenos Aires, the weak economy of the country, and the poor condition of some of the stadia.

Scotland were the only qualifiers from Britain, England having failed to qualify for a second time. The two newcomers to the semi-final stages were Tunisia and Iran. The format was precisely the same as in 1974, and the countries were grouped as follows:

Group 1
Argentina, France, Hungary and Italy

Group 2
Mexico, Poland, Tunisia and West Germany

Group 3
Austria, Brazil, Spain and Sweden

Group 4
Holland, Iran, Peru and Scotland

The Argentinian manager, Menotti, faced problems building a team because so many players had moved abroad, mainly to Spanish clubs. He had recalled Kempes, however, who had matured into one of the most dangerous goal-scorers in the world. The Dutch team was much diminished from that which had finished as runners-up in the last series, most notably because of Cruyff's decision not to take part. They still had Rep,

Rensenbrink and Neeskens, however, and a new manager, Ernst Happel. West Germany were without Franz Beckenbauer, Muller and Overath, but still had a team which looked capable of retaining the World Cup.

There were no real surprises in the qualifying group matches, although it was thought that France would qualify with their open style of play but odd-goal defeats against both Italy and Argentina ruined their chance. In group two, West Germany nearly paid the penalty for being too complacent against Tunisia, and while they enjoyed the upper hand for most of the game, they could not break down the newcomers' resolute defence. West Germany were group runners-up to Poland, but the Germans grumbled about their manager's tactics and boredom at the team's training camp. Austria and Brazil went through from group three, although the latter were below their form of previous tournaments. Spain were eliminated, mainly because they played reasonably well as individuals but badly as a team. Holland and Peru took the last two places, with the Dutch just scraping through with a superior goal average to that of Scotland. Scotland, therefore, went out on goal difference, humbled by Peru, and further humiliated when Willie Johnston failed a drugs test and was sent home.

At the next stage, Holland won their group and entered the Final for the second time in succession. Brazil finished runners-up to Argentina in group B. The surprise in that group came from Peru who, after winning their early group with an unbeaten record, collapsed at this stage without getting either a point or a goal. Their last game was against Argentina, who needed to win 4–0 to reach the Final. With their partisan crowd urging them on, Argentina made it 6–0 with an exhilarating display of football.

The Final saw Argentina competing for the first time

in the last four tournaments, but they were playing a Dutch side eager to go one better than in Munich four years earlier. The first half saw the Argentinians very much on top, with almost continuous attacking moves which eventually got them the vital first goal by Kempes. After the interval, the Dutch settled in and proceeded to dictate the play. With nine minutes to go, they equalised through Nanninga. With thirty seconds to go, the Argentinian off-side trap went wrong and Rensenbrink, with only the keeper to beat, hit the post. In extra time, Argentina found some reserve energy while the Dutch tired, and the home side scored twice to clinch a memorable victory, much to the delight of their supporters.

The attendance at the Final had been approximately 77,000, which brought the total for the 38 games to 1.6 million, giving an average of over 42,000 per match. Overall, 102 goals were scored with Kempes the leader, netting six. Over 6700 press passes had been issued, confirming the continuing increase in coverage and popularity of the World Cup.

Results

First pool matches
Group 1

Argentina 2, Hungary 1	Italy 3, Hungary 1
Italy 2, France 1	Italy 1, Argentina 0
Argentina 2, France 1	France 3, Hungary 1

	P	W	D	L	F	A	Pts
Italy	3	3	0	0	6	2	6
Argentina	3	2	0	1	4	3	4
France	3	1	0	2	5	5	2
Hungary	3	0	0	3	3	8	0

Group 2

West Germany 0, Poland 0	West Germany 6, Mexico 0
Tunisia 3, Mexico 1	Poland 3, Mexico 1
Poland 1, Tunisia 0	West Germany 0, Tunisia 0

	P	W	D	L	F	A	Pts
Poland	3	2	1	0	4	1	5
West Germany	3	1	2	0	6	0	4
Tunisia	3	1	1	1	3	2	3
Mexico	3	0	0	3	2	12	0

Group 3

Austria 2, Spain 1	Brazil 0, Spain 0
Sweden 1, Brazil 1	Spain 1, Sweden 0
Austria 1, Sweden 0	Brazil 1, Austria 0

	P	W	D	L	F	A	Pts
Austria	3	2	0	1	3	2	4
Brazil	3	1	2	1	2	1	4
Spain	3	1	1	1	2	2	3
Sweden	3	0	1	2 —	1	3	1

Group 4

Peru 3, Scotland 1	Holland 0, Peru 0
Holland 3, Iran 0	Peru 4, Iran 1
Scotland 1, Iran 1	Scotland 3, Holland 2

	P	W	D	L	F	A	Pts
Peru	3	2	1	0	7	2	5
Holland	3	1	1	1	5	3	3
Scotland	3	1	1	1	5	6	3
Iran	3	0	1	2	2	8	1

Second pool matches
Group A

Italy 0, West Germany 0	Austria 3, West Germany 2
Holland 5, Austria 1	Holland 2, Italy 1
Italy 1, Austria 0	Holland 2, West Germany 2

	P	W	D	L	F	A	Pts
Holland	3	2	1	0	9	4	5
Italy	3	1	1	1	2	2	3
West Germany	3	0	2	1	4	5	2
Austria	3	1	0	2	4	8	2

Group B

Argentina 2, Poland 0	Poland 1, Peru 0
Brazil 3, Peru 0	Brazil 3, Poland 1
Argentina 0, Brazil 0	Argentina 6, Peru 0

	P	W	D	L	F	A	Pts
Argentina	3	2	1	0	8	0	5
Brazil	3	2	1	0	6	1	5
Poland	3	1	0	2	2	5	2
Peru	3	0	0	3	0	10	0

Third place match
Brazil 2
Nelinho, Dirceu

Italy 1
Causio

Final
Argentina 3
(after extra time)
Fillol; Olguin, Galvan,
Passarella, Tarantini; Ardiles
(Larrosa), Gallego, Kempes;
Bertoni, Luque, Ortiz
(Houseman).

Holland 1

Jongbloed; Krol, Poortvliet,
Brandts, Jansen (Suurbier);
van de Kerkhof, W.,
Neeskens, Haan; Rep
(Nanninga), Rensenbrink,
van de Kerkhof, R.

SCORERS
Kempes (2), Bertoni
(HT 1/0 FT 1/1)

SCORER
Nanninga

SPAIN 1982

There was little objection to Spain as a venue for the twelfth World Cup, although the size of the entry caused some organisational problems. Responding to the demands of Third World countries, FIFA increased the number of entries by 50 per cent to twenty-four. It took fifty-two countries 306 games, and very nearly 800 goals, to sort themselves out into the final twenty-four. The tournament kicked off on 26 March 1980, when Eire beat Cyprus at home 3–2. Twenty-two months later, New Zealand beat China 2–1 in a dramatic play-off in Singapore, to clinch the final place in Spain. For many teams, not least England, it was a long, nail-biting road.

The system of retaining second-round groups was maintained, which affected the standard of play in that countries were content to play draws. The competition was divided into six first-round groups of four countries, the top two of which progressed to four second-round groups of three countries. A knock-out basis then applied as each group winner went into a semi-final tie, with the winners going through to the Final and the losers to the third-place match. The countries were grouped as below:

Group 1
Cameroon, Italy, Peru and Poland

Group 2
Algeria, Austria, Chile and West Germany

Group 3
Argentina, Belgium, El Salvador and Hungary

Group 4
Czechoslovakia, England, France and Kuwait

Group 5
Honduras, Northern Ireland, Spain and Yugoslavia

Group 6
Brazil, New Zealand, Scotland and Russia

It was hard to find favourites, but the West Germans looked good. Paul Breitner, the captain, was a dynamic midfield player; Littbarski was quick and clever and European Footballer of the Year; Karl Heinz Rummenigge ranked among the best strikers in the game. Argentina were still under the capable management of Menotti, who now had a new weapon in the thick-thighed shape of Diego Maradona. Brazil, with an abundance of midfield players including Zico, Socrates and Falcao, were encouraged by their manager Tele Santana to attack and express themselves. Italy had played badly on their way to Spain, but Enzo Berzot drafted in some newcomers including Bruno Conti, the diminutive Roma winger.

England made a very good start against France in Bilbao, scoring after only twenty-seven seconds, the quickest goal in the story of the competition, and they ran out clear 3–1 winners in the end. Unfortunately for England's chances in the competition overall, neither Trevor Brooking nor Kevin Keegan played, and neither was to do so until the very last match. Hungary beat El Salvador 10–1, the highest World Cup score to date, emphasising the difference in class between the emerging soccer nations and the traditionally stronger countries. Group two began with the biggest surprise of the tournament as Algeria beat West Germany 2–1, with the latter recovering to beat Chile 4–1 in the next match. Northern Ireland played perhaps their most outstanding World Cup game ever when they beat Spain 1–0, Gerry Armstrong scoring two minutes into the second half, to qualify for the next round as top of group five. They overcame a hostile crowd, dubious refereeing, the intense heat, and even a player sent off.

The second-round qualifiers were grouped as follows:

Group A
Belgium, Poland and Russia

Group B
England, Spain and West Germany

Group C
Argentina, Brazil and Italy

Group D
Austria, France and Northern Ireland

Group A began with Boniek of Poland scoring a hat-trick against Belgium on the Poles' route to the semi-finals. When England met Spain in group B, they required a 2–0 victory, but failed to score and their opponents went through instead. Rossi was the star of group C, returning to the Italian side after a two-year exile following a bribery scandal; his brilliant hat-trick against Brazil took his team to the semi-finals. France won a decisive game in group D, beating Northern Ireland 4–1 to end that country's brave challenge.

Italy beat Poland 2–0 at Barcelona, but the encounter between France and Germany in the other semi-final was the most thrilling match of the 1982 series. Platini was in fine form, equalising from a penalty spot after Littbarski had given West Germany the lead. The German goalkeeper, Schumacher, found instant fame – but for the wrong reasons, as he committed one of the most dreadful fouls in the World Cup, thundering into Batison and smashing him to the ground, leaving the Frenchman minus two teeth and extremely badly hurt. As Schumacher, remarkably, remained on the field, this incident probably contributed to West Germany's ultimate victory, 5–4 on penalties after extra time.

The Final, between Italy and West Germany, was notable for Cabrini becoming the first player to miss a penalty kick in a World Cup Final. The Italians scored three times after this, however, goals coming from Rossi, Tardelli and Altobelli, with Breitner pulling one back for the Germans in the eighty-second minute. Italy, therefore, became the first European country to have won the World Cup three times.

Results

First pool matches
Group 1
Italy 0, Poland 0   Cameroon 0, Poland 0
Cameroon 0, Peru 0   Poland 5, Peru 1
Italy 1, Peru 1   Italy 1, Cameroon 1

	P	W	D	L	F	A	Pts
Poland	3	1	2	0	5	1	4
Italy	3	0	3	0	2	2	3
Cameroon	3	0	3	0	1	1	3
Peru	3	0	2	1	2	6	2

Group 2
Algeria 2, West Germany 1   Algeria 0, Austria 2
Austria 1, Chile 0   Algeria 3, Chile 2
West Germany 4, Chile 1   West Germany 1, Austria 0

	P	W	D	L	F	A	Pts
West Germany	3	2	0	1	6	3	4
Austria	3	2	0	1	3	1	4
Algeria	3	2	0	1	5	5	4
Chile	3	0	0	3	3	8	0

Group 3
Argentina 0, Belgium 1   Belgium 1, El Salvador 0
Hungary 10, El Salvador 1   Belgium 1, Hungary 1
Argentina 4, Hungary 1   Argentina 2, El Salvador 0

	P	W	D	L	F	A	Pts
Belgium	3	2	1	0	3	1	5
Argentina	3	2	0	1	6	2	4
Hungary	3	1	1	1	12	6	3
El Salvador	3	0	0	3	1	13	0

Group 4

England 3, France 1

France 4, Kuwait 1

Czechoslovakia 1, Kuwait 1

France 1, Czechoslovakia 1

England 2, Czechoslovakia 0

England 1, Kuwait 0

	P	W	D	L	F	A	Pts
England	3	3	0	0	6	1	6
France	3	1	1	1	6	5	3
Czechoslovakia	3	0	2	1	2	4	2
Kuwait	3	0	1	2	2	6	1

Group 5

Spain 1, Honduras 1

Honduras 1, N. Ireland 1

Yugoslavia 0, N. Ireland 0

Honduras 0, Yugoslavia 1

Spain 2, Yugoslavia 1

Spain 0, N. Ireland 1

	P	W	D	L	F	A	Pts
N. Ireland	3	1	2	0	2	1	4
Spain	3	1	1	0	3	3	3
Yugoslavia	3	1	1	1	2	2	3
Honduras	3	0	2	1	2	3	2

Group 6

Brazil 2, Russia 1

Russia 3, New Zealand 0

Scotland 5, New Zealand 2

Scotland 2, Russia 2

Brazil 4, Scotland 1

Brazil 4, New Zealand 0

	P	W	D	L	F	A	Pts
Brazil	3	3	0	0	10	2	6
Russia	3	1	1	1	6	4	3
Scotland	3	1	1	1	8	8	3
New Zealand	3	0	0	3	2	12	0

Second pool matches
Group A

Poland 3, Belgium 0

Russia 0, Poland 0

Belgium 0, Russia 1

	P	W	D	L	F	A	Pts
Poland	2	1	1	0	3	0	3
Russia	2	1	1	0	1	0	3
Belgium	2	0	0	2	0	4	0

Group B

West Germany 0, England 0   Spain 0, England 0
West Germany 2, Spain 1

	P	W	D	L	F	A	Pts
West Germany	2	1	1	0	2	1	3
England	2	0	2	0	0	0	2
Spain	2	0	1	1	1	2	1

Group C

Italy 2, Argentina 1   Italy 3, Brazil 2
Brazil 3, Argentina 1

	P	W	D	L	F	A	Pts
Italy	2	2	0	0	5	3	4
Brazil	2	1	0	1	5	4	2
Argentina	2	0	0	2	2	5	0

Group D

France 1, Austria 0   France 4, Northern Ireland 1
Austria 2, Northern Ireland 2

	P	W	D	L	F	A	Pts
France	2	2	0	0	5	1	4
Austria	2	0	1	1	2	3	1
N. Ireland	2	0	1	1	3	6	1

Semi-finals

Italy 2   **Poland 0**
Rossi (2)

West Germany 3   **France 3**
Littbarski, Rummenigge,   Platini (penalty), Trésor,
Fischer   Giresse
(after extra time)
West Germany won 5–4 on penalties.

Third place match
Poland 3   **France 2**
Szarmach, Majewski,   Girard, Couriol
Kupcewicz

Final

Italy 3	**West Germany 1**
Zoff; Scirea; Bergomi,	Schumacher; Stielike; Kaltz,
Gentile, Collovati, Cabrini;	K-H. Foerster, B. Foerster,
Tardelli, Oriali; Conti, Rossi,	Briegel; Dremmler
Graziani (Altobelli, Conti).	(Hrubesch), Breitner;
	Littbarski, Rummenigge
	(H. Muller), Fischer.

SCORERS	SCORER
Rossi, Tardelli, Altobelli	Breitner
(HT 0/0)	

MEXICO 1986

Columbia had been the original choice of venue for the thirteenth World Cup, but they could not raise sufficient funds and so FIFA selected Mexico instead. Although severe earthquakes shook the area in 1985, the stadia were not affected and Mexico therefore became the first country to host the World Cup for a second time.

The organisation of the tournament was changed back again to a knock-out basis after the first round, with the top two from each of the six first-round groups of four progressing to the second round, together with the best third-placed teams. In the event of a stalemate at the end of any of the knock-out games, provision was made for extra time followed by a penalty shoot-out as necessary. The first-round groupings were:

Group A
Argentina, Bulgaria, Italy and South Korea

Group B
Belgium, Iraq, Mexico and Paraguay

Group C
Canada, France, Hungary and USSR

Group D
Algeria, Brazil, Northern Ireland and Spain

Group E
Denmark, Scotland, Uruguay and West Germany

Group F
England, Morocco, Poland and Portugal

Argentina were always going to be formidable opponents because of Diego Maradona, who was in a class of his own with the sort of play which could win a match in five minutes of blinding skill. England were confident because they had qualified in real style, winning four and drawing four of their eight games, scoring 21 goals and conceding only two. France and Brazil both possessed good individuals able to play within established team patterns. The West Germans, although rather dour and defensive, had proved over the years that they were capable of progressing all the way.

The competition began on 31 May 1986 in the Azteca Stadium, Mexico City, when the champions, Italy, played a good opening game against Bulgaria which ended in a 1–1 draw. The score was the same when Italy played the Argentinians in the second game, leaving the Italians requiring a victory against South Korea to make the second round. In that match, Altobelli scored all three goals in Italy's 3–2 victory. Mexico topped group B with Hugo Sanchez playing some classy football. The major surprise in group C was USSR's 6–0 thrashing of Hungary, the Russians winning the group to qualify, along with France, for the next stage.

The teams in group F had to contend with extraordinarily intense heat and humidity. After a poor start, losing to Portugal and managing only a draw against Morocco, England made important changes for the crucial match against Poland. Reid, Trevor Steven,

Hodge and Beardsley provided the transformation and a 3–0 victory, with Gary Lineker scoring the first World Cup hat-trick for England since Geoff Hurst's in the 1966 Final.

The competition then moved to the knock-out rounds which provided some high-scoring matches, including Belgium's 4–3 win over Russia, Brazil's 4–0 trouncing of Poland, and Spain's 5–1 defeat of the Danes.

The quarter-finals provided two classic ties, Brazil *v* France and Argentina *v* England, with Mexico *v* West Germany and Belgium *v* Spain providing the other matches. Although Careca shot Brazil ahead after fifteen minutes, Platini equalised. With a quarter of an hour to go, Zico came on as substitute and almost immediately took a penalty, which he missed. As a result the game went into extra time without further goals, and France won the penalty shoot-out 4–3.

England *versus* Argentina was played under the shadow of the Falklands War, and proved to be a tense occasion. The game was at stalemate until the fiftieth minute, when Maradona chased a lofted back pass, challenged Shilton, and pushed the ball into the net with what seemed to be his hand. Despite protests, the goal was allowed to stand and it was followed five minutes later by a second from Maradona, this time one of the greatest in the history of the competition. He picked up the ball on the half-way line and dribbled past three defenders before knocking the ball past Shilton. In the eightieth minute, substitute Barnes crossed for Lineker to head into the Argentinian net, a feat which he almost repeated three minutes from the end. England had left it too late.

There was less excitement in the semi-finals, West Germany winning through by solid defending and deter-mination. The scene was set for confrontation in the

Final against the other qualifiers, Argentina. Jose Luis Brown gave the Argentinians the lead when he took advantage of a bad mistake by goalkeeper Schumacher, and Valdano added a second. Then Rummenigge pulled a goal back, and Voller equalised in quick succession. But Maradona had the last word; he split the West German defence with a superb ball which Burrachaga picked up to score the winner.

Argentina had won their second world title and Maradona was the man of the tournament, although England's Gary Lineker finished up as top scorer. Bobby Robson said afterwards: 'Walking away from the Azteca Stadium, I could hold my head up high. We were so close to being the best – only one disputed goal away from the world champions.'

Results

Pool 1

Bulgaria 1, Italy 1		South Korea 1, Bulgaria 1			
Argentina 3, South Korea 1		Argentina 2, Bulgaria 0			
Italy 1, Argentina 1		South Korea 2, Italy 3			

	P	W	D	L	F	A	Pts
Argentina	3	2	1	0	6	2	5
Italy	3	1	2	0	5	4	4
Bulgaria	3	0	2	1	2	4	2
South Korea	3	0	1	2	4	7	1

Pool 2

Belgium 1, Mexico 2	Iraq 1, Belgium 2
Paraguay 1, Iraq 0	Paraguay 2, Belgium 2
Mexico 1, Paraguay 1	Iraq 0, Mexico 1

	P	W	D	L	F	A	Pts
Mexico	3	2	1	0	4	2	5
Paraguay	3	1	2	0	4	3	4
Belgium	3	1	1	1	5	5	3
Iraq	3	0	0	3	1	4	0

Pool 3

USSR 6, Hungary 0   Hungary 2, Canada 0
Canada 0, France 1   Hungary 0, France 3
France 1, USSR 1   USSR 2, Canada 0

	P	W	D	L	F	A	Pts
USSR	3	2	1	0	9	1	5
France	3	2	1	0	5	1	5
Hungary	3	1	0	2	2	9	2
Canada	3	0	0	3	0	5	0

Pool 4

Spain 0, Brazil 1   Brazil 1, Algeria 0
Algeria 1, N. Ireland 1   Algeria 0, Spain 3
N. Ireland 1, Spain 2   N. Ireland 0, Brazil 3

	P	W	D	L	F	A	Pts
Brazil	3	3	0	0	5	0	6
Spain	3	2	0	1	5	2	4
N. Ireland	3	0	1	2	2	6	1
Algeria	3	0	1	2	1	5	1

Pool 5

Uruguay 1, W. Germany 1   W. Germany 2, Scotland 1
Scotland 0, Denmark 1   Scotland 0, Uruguay 0
Denmark 6, Uruguay 1   Denmark 2, W. Germany 0

	P	W	D	L	F	A	Pts
Denmark	3	3	0	0	9	1	6
W. Germany	3	1	1	1	3	4	3
Uruguay	3	0	2	1	2	7	2
Scotland	3	0	1	2	1	3	1

Pool 6

Morocco 0, Poland 0   Poland 1, Portugal 0
Portugal 1, England 0   England 3, Poland 0
England 0, Morocco 0   Portugal 1, Morocco 3

	P	W	D	L	F	A	Pts
Morocco	3	1	2	0	3	1	4
England	3	1	1	1	3	1	3
Poland	3	1	1	1	1	3	3
Portugal	3	1	0	2	2	4	2

Second round

Argentina 1, Uruguay 0
Paraguay 0, England 3
USSR 3, Belgium 4
(after extra time)
Spain 5, Denmark 1

Brazil 4, Poland 0
Italy 0, France 2
Morocco 0, W. Germany 1
Mexico 2, Bulgaria 0

Quarter-finals

Argentina 2   **England 1**

Belgium 1   **Spain 1**
(after extra time)
(Belgium won 5–4 on penalties)

Brazil 1   **France 1**
(after extra time)
(France won 4–3 on penalties)

W. Germany 0   **Mexico 0**
(after extra time)
(W. Germany won 4–1 on penalties)

Semi-finals

Argentina 2   **Belgium 0**
Maradona (2)

W. Germany 2   **France 0**
Brehme, Voller

Third place match

France 4   **Belgium 2**
Ferreri, Papin, Genghini,   Ceulemans, Claesen
Amoros (penalty)
(after extra time)

Final

Argentina 3   **W. Germany 2**
Pumpido; Ruggeri, Brown,   Schumacher; Brehme,
Cuciuffo; Giusti, Enrique,   Jakobs, Foerster (K.H.),
Batista, Burrachaga,   Berthold; Matthaus, Magath
(Trobbiani); Olaricoechea,   (Hoeness), Eder; Briegel,
Valdano, Maradona.   Rummenigge, Allofs (Voller).

SCORERS   SCORERS
Brown, Valdano, Burrachaga   Rummenigge, Voller
(HT 1/0)

FIFTY ALL-TIME GREATS

CARLOS ALBERTO – BRAZIL

Alberto captained the brilliant Brazilian team that won the Jules Rimet Trophy outright in Mexico in 1970. His adventurous, overlapping run from a right-back base was a feature of the Brazilian approach play, and his industry and invention were rewarded in the Final when he scored Brazil's fourth goal against Italy. Born in 1945, he became recognised as one of the world's most outstanding defenders while a club-mate to Pelé at Santos. He was skipper at Santos before following Pelé's path to the United States, where he became a popular player with New York Cosmos.

TAVARES AMARILDO – BRAZIL

An understudy to the great Pelé, the twenty-two-year-old Amarildo thought he was going to the 1962 Finals in Chile just for the ride, but when Pelé pulled a muscle in the second match of the tournament, Amarildo was suddenly promoted to the key position in Brazil's attack. He answered the challenge by scoring two goals against Spain in his World Cup debut. The reason he slotted so smoothly into the team was that he had his Botafogo club-mates Garrincha, Didì and Zagalo to support him. Nicknamed the 'White Pelé', Amarildo went on to help Brazil retain the World Cup, scoring the first goal in their 3–1 victory over Czechoslovakia in the Final.

OSVALDO ARDILES – ARGENTINA

This silky smooth midfield schemer was one of the chief architects of Argentina's 1978 World Cup triumph. The son of a lawyer, he had to choose between law and football. He passed his law exams but chose to concentrate on earning a living with his feet, and quickly established himself as one of the most accomplished players in South America while playing club football for Hurracan. Ardiles was twenty-five when he made the amazing decision to join Tottenham Hotspur in a £325,000 transfer just weeks after helping Argentina to win the World Cup, and he soon won the hearts of English football fans with his skills and sportsmanship. Now that his playing career has virtually ended, Osvaldo has stayed in England to manage Swindon Town.

ALAN BALL – ENGLAND

Alan Ball, playing the game of his life, helped push England to the extra-time victory against Germany in the 1966 World Cup Final at Wembley. At twenty-one he was the baby of the England team, but he gave Germany's Karl Heinz Schnellinger a chasing he is unlikely to forget. A red-headed terrier of a player, Ball had been the midfield motivator for a host of English League clubs before entering management, but he will be best remembered for his exploits with England. The son of an ex-professional footballer, he was born at Farnworth, Lancashire, on 5 May 1945. He won 72 caps, skippered England six times, and played in four World Cup ties in 1966 plus four more in 1970, including an appearance as substitute against Czechoslovakia.

GORDON BANKS – ENGLAND

Banks rivals Russia's legendary Lev Yashin as the greatest ever goalkeeper to play World Cup football. In 1966, Banks equalled the record of conceding only three goals in a full span of World Cup Final matches. A save from a downward header by Pelé in the 1970 tournament is still talked about as the finest reaction save ever witnessed. Banks, born in Sheffield on 30 December 1937, played 73 times for England from 1963 to 1972, when tragically he lost the sight of his right eye in a car crash. The opposition failed to put the ball past him in 35 of his England appearances. He conceded only four goals in nine World Cup Final matches. When he missed the 1970 quarter-final against West Germany because of a stomach ailment, England's chances of retaining the Cup virtually disappeared with him.

FRANZ BECKENBAUER – WEST GERMANY

This elegant player won 103 international caps between 1965 and 1977, when he accepted New York Cosmos' offer of a $2.5 million contract. He had established himself as a regular member of the 1966 West German team by the age of twenty. Despite such tender years, his creative ability led manager Helmut Schoen to give him a man-to-man marking job on Bobby Charlton in the Final. Revenge for that defeat was sweet, as Beckenbauer scored the goal which beat an England side in 1968, scored again in the 1970 World Cup victory, and captained the team which beat them again on the way to winning the 1972 European Championship. By then he had moved from midfield to an attacking-sweeper role, often scoring himself. He later became West Germany's manager, carefully playing down the team's chances in the 1986 World Cup competition before leading them all the way to the Final.

ROMEO BENETTI – ITALY

Born 29 October 1945, a much-transferred midfield player and full of hard running, Benetti loved to build up attacks. When Italy played England in November 1976, he layed off a pinpoint cross from which Bettega scored. A rugged tackler, he played in the 1974 World Cup.

OVAR BERGMARK – SWEDEN

Ovar was a solid and thoughtful right-back whose playing career reached its peak in 1958 when he played for Sweden against Brazil in the World Cup Final in Stockholm. It was one of 94 international appearances he made for Sweden. Twelve years later, in his new role of manager, he led Sweden to the 1970 Finals after they had topped a qualifying group which included hot favourites France.

ROBERTO BETTEGA – ITALY

Born 27 December 1950, his goal against England in their match in Rome was described by Bill Shankly as being the 'goal of the century'. It was a high, diving header that rocketed into the net after a crisp build-up. At his peak, Bettega was one of the best forwards in European football.

JOSEF BOZIC – HUNGARY

Born in 1925, Bozic was an attacking wing-half in the 'Magical Magyars' team that won the Olympic title in 1952, thrashed England 6–3 at Wembley in 1953, but finished runners-up to West Germany in the 1954 World Cup Final, a match they were expected to win easily. Bozic, now a Member of the Hungarian House of Representatives, played 100 times for Hungary between 1947 and 1962, and his flair and fire provided an important midfield motivating force.

PAUL BREITNER – WEST GERMANY

One of the inventive full-backs of modern times, this highly individualistic character established himself as a world star with Bayern Munich in West Germany, and later displayed his artistic talent in midfield with Real Madrid before returning to Bayern as captain and resuming his international career. Breitner was a key man in the 1982 Finals in Spain, marshalling the West German attacking force from a midfield command post.

Born in Bavaria on 5 September 1951, he first came to international prominence when helping Germany to win the Nations Cup in 1972. His attacking runs down the left flank from his base at left-back were a feature of his country's 1974 World Cup triumph, where his contribution included three crucial goals. Off the field, Breitner has worked extensively with handicapped children and has also adopted a Vietnamese orphan.

BOBBY CHARLTON – ENGLAND

A non-playing member of England's 1958 squad, after surviving the horrific Munich air crash Bobby went on to play in three World Cup Finals tournaments. He had his most satisfying moments in 1966, when he was the chief architect in England's triumph. He was born at Ashington, the largest pit village in England, on 11 October 1937, and during his distinguished career won winner's medals in the World Cup 1966, European Cup 1968, League Championship 1957, 1965, 1967, and the FA Cup in 1963. He scored a record 49 goals for England, was voted European Footballer of the Year in 1966, captained Manchester United's 1968 European Cup-winning team, and shares with Bobby Moore the record of playing in 14 World Cup Final matches. He played all four matches in 1962 as an outside-left, and had switched to a deep-lying, schemer role by the time of the 1966 campaign, when his contribution to England's success, apart from a procession of precise passes, included three superbly struck goals, two of them against Portugal in the semi-final. He then set a new 'caps-collection' record of 106 in his final cap-match against West Germany in the 1970 quarter-final, during which he was substituted before England's nose-dive to a 3–2 defeat.

JACK CHARLTON – ENGLAND

Jack followed his younger brother, Bobby, into the England team as a dominating centre-half, winning 35 caps after beginning his international career at the age of twenty-nine. Like Bobby, he played in all six of England's 1966 World Cup matches, and also like his younger brother his last international appearance was in the 1970 Finals. He played just one match in Mexico, replacing Brian Labone in the 1–0 defeat of Czechoslovakia. Born at Ashington on 8 May 1936, he played in a record 629 League matches for Leeds between 1953 and 1973. Footballer of the Year in 1967, succeeding brother Bobby, he was elected Manager of the Year in 1974 after steering Middlesbrough back into the First Division. He later took over at Sheffield Wednesday and had a spell at Newcastle United before his appointment as manager of the Republic of Ireland team.

JOHANN CRUYFF – HOLLAND

Elected European Footballer of the Year three times – 1971, 1973 and 1974 – Cruyff was a player of immense skills and speed. This Dutch master skilfully steered Holland to the runners-up position in the 1974 World Cup Final. Born within goal-kicking distance of the Ajax ground in Amsterdam on 25 April 1947, he developed into a stunning striker who could also scheme goals. He, more than anyone, was behind the Ajax rise as the 'Kings of Europe'. It was significant that when he moved to Barcelona in 1973, the Dutch team was no longer the same formidable force. He orchestrated the Ajax victory in the European Cup three times, and he then inspired Barcelona to the Spanish Championship. After a short retirement, he resumed his career in the United States of America.

EUSEBIO – PORTUGAL

Born in Mozambique in 1942, he was snapped up from FC Lorenco Marques by Benfica of Lisbon in 1961, and won the first of more than 60 international caps in his first season with his new club. Nicknamed the 'Black Panther', he could move through defences at a sprint speed and had a tremendous right-foot shot. He was voted European Footballer of the Year in 1961, and was the World Cup tournament's top scorer in 1966 when his nine goals lifted Portugal to a sensational semi-final place against England. He finished his playing career in the United States of America.

GLACINTO FACCHETTI – ITALY

Italian Footballer of the Year in 1968, this tall, elegant left-back was an adventurous player who knocked in many vital goals for Inter Milan and Italy. He was born at Treviglio on 18 July 1942 and signed for Inter Milan at the age of eighteen, becoming a key member of a defence which stifled the life out of the best club attacks in Europe. His personal peak came in 1970 when he captained the Italian team that reached the World Cup Final against Brazil. Facchetti also played in the 1966 and 1974 World Cup tournaments.

JUST FONTAINE – FRANCE

Born in Marrakesh, Morocco in 1933, the Frenchman Fontaine had been struggling to win a permanent place in the French attack during the build-up to the 1958 Finals in Sweden. He had been an international player in 1956, but rarely showed his club form at international level. It all came right for him, however, in Sweden when he collected a record 13 goals as he helped to power France into the best ever third place. His haul included four goals in the third-place play-off against West Germany, and a hat-trick in his World Cup debut against Paraguay. He played club football for Nice and Rheims, and was top league scorer in France in 1958 and in 1960, before a twice-broken leg brought a premature end to his career. He was briefly a member of the French national team and served as President of the Players' Union. Fontaine's prolific partnership with French idol Raymond Copo was considered one of the most potent pairings in French history.

GERSON – BRAZIL

A master strategist, Gerson was the player who plotted Brazil's triumph in the 1970 World Cup. His precise passing from midfield gave the Brazilians drive and direction, and he also packed a powerful finishing shot, as he proved with a spectacular goal in the 1970 Final against Italy. Born at Niteroi on the Bay of Rio in 1941, he first came into world prominence in the 1960 Olympic Soccer Tournament in Italy. He failed to make an impression in his one World Cup appearance in the 1966 Finals in England, but four years later he emerged as Brazil's key midfield schemer. Criticised for a lack of enthusiasm in training and for smoking an alleged forty cigarettes a day, Gerson had a bitter dispute with the manager of the Flamengo club and was transferred to their Rio neighbours Botafogo. He won 84 caps and wound down his distinguished career with Sao Paulo when a broken ankle forced his retirement in 1973.

RUUD GULLIT – HOLLAND

Although born in Amsterdam he elected to start his career with Haarlem, serving them for four years before joining Feyenoord in 1982, by which time he was an established international. He won a championship medal in 1984, adding two more in successive seasons after moving to PSV Eindhoven. In the summer of 1987, the year he was voted Footballer of the Year, AC Milan paid an amazing £5.5 million for him. An outstanding all-round footballer who can play as sweeper or in midfield, Ruud is also a colourful personality who will, undoubtedly, make a big impression in this year's World Cup tournament.

GEOFF HURST – ENGLAND

The name Geoff Hurst was cemented into World Cup history the day he scored the glorious hat-trick that won the Jules Rimet Trophy for England at Wembley in 1966. He also scored the crucial winning goal against Argentina in the quarter-finals, when he came into the attack for his World Cup debut. The son of a professional footballer, Hurst was born at Ashton-under-Lyme on 8 December 1941. He netted 180 League goals for West Ham, and 22 for Stoke, before playing briefly for West Bromwich Albion. Hurst then became player–manager for Telford United, a stepping-stone to a job as manager of Chelsea with whom he had a brief, eventful association.

PAT JENNINGS – NORTHERN IRELAND

Universally recognised as being one of the best keepers in Europe, Pat gained his first cap while still with

Watford. He was plunged into the First Division with Spurs, and was a pillar of the successful Tottenham side of the late 1960s and early 1970s. Utterly fearless and full of spectacular saves, Pat has a huge pair of hands and his trademark of leaping, one-handed catches was spectacular to watch. His positional sense was superb, and he was not afraid to make excursions out of his goal area. His greatest moments were ahead of him as he saw Arsenal to three consecutive Cup Finals, from 1978 to 1980, as he was to help Northern Ireland to the World Cup Finals in Spain and Mexico. The latter provided a perfect end to his career after a short spell with Tottenham where he had returned to keep fit for the occasion. Jennings made his record 109th appearance against Brazil at the age of forty-one.

KEVIN KEEGAN – ENGLAND

Born 14 February 1951, Kevin gave enormous pleasure to people all over Europe with his determined running and attack, weaving first one way and then the other. He had much to do with the success of Liverpool in the 1970s, and was widely thought of as being the most 'Latin' of English players. In the twilight of his career, he helped Newcastle United to win promotion to the First Division.

MARIO KEMPES – ARGENTINA

Kempes turned the 1978 World Cup into a showcase for his glittering talents, scoring the most goals in the tournament and doing more than anyone to capture the world championship for Argentina. Born in Cordoba in

1955, he played in the 1974 World Cup Finals as a nineteen-year-old striker, but was overshadowed by players such as Housemann and Brindisi. His game flourished after he left his local club, Rosario Central, and joined Valencia in Spain in 1976. He was top scorer for Valencia in his first two seasons, and the Spanish club was so pleased with his form that they signed him to a new five-year contract before he returned to Argentina for the 1978 World Cup. He looked a £3 million player in the Finals, continually arresting the eye with his speed of thought and action, balance and decidedly accurate finish. He was equally accurate in midfield or in any front-line position, and was particularly devastating when in partnership with Luque. Fittingly, it was his two goals which clinched the 3–1 victory over Holland in the Final. In 1981 he returned to Argentina to join River Plate.

GRZEGORZ LATO – POLAND

Lato signalled his arrival as a world-class player with his superb performances for Poland in the 1974 World Cup qualifying matches, when England were among the teams 'Pole-axed'! Born on 8 April 1950, he helped Stal Mielic win the Polish League Championship before joining the international team for the World Cup Finals in West Germany. The Poles had lost their star forward Lubanski with injury, but Lato compensated for his absence by growing in stature, and his strong right-foot shooting brought him the tournament's top haul of seven goals, the last of which earned Poland third place. He was prominent again for Poland in the 1978 Finals, this time more of a goal-maker than a taker. Although scoring only two goals in six matches, he troubled every defence he faced with his acceleration and deft touches.

GARY LINEKER – ENGLAND

You have to go back to the days of Nat Lofthouse to find a rate to equal Lineker's 19 goals in his first 20 starts for England, and the Tottenham forward did it against tight, modern defences. Gary began his career with home club Leicester City before moving to Everton and, subsequently, Barcelona to join manager Terry Venables. When Venables moved to Spurs, Gary eventually followed. It was a move to Everton in 1985, soon after he had forced his way into the England team, which confirmed Lineker's outstanding qualities. He has the speed to break clear from defenders and is a lethal finisher either one-on-one with the goalkeeper or inside the six-yard box, where he has the knack of being in the right place at the right time. His thrilling form was taken to the 1986 World Cup, where he emerged as the tournament's leading scorer with six goals, including a first-half hat-trick against Poland which saved England's blushes in the first round.

SEPP MAIER – WEST GERMANY

Played in the tournaments of 1970 and 1974, in both of which he distinguished himself by his bravery and skill. A member of the Bayern Munich team which gave him his vastly successful career in European club football, he was very much part of the club's successes in the mid 1970s.

DIEGO MARADONA – ARGENTINA

Unrivalled as the current No. 1 player in the world. Unfortunately, most English people will remember him more for his 'hand-of-God' goal against England in the last World Cup competition than for his undoubted

ability. Born on 30 October 1960, Maradona made his league debut at fifteen and played for Argentina as a seventeen-year-old substitute in a 5–1 win over Hungary in 1977. Considered by manager Cesar Menotti as too young for the 1978 World Cup, Maradona was dropped from the squad on the eve of the Finals. He has played club soccer in Europe since 1982, first for Barcelona and then for Napoli, who paid a then world record £5 million for his services. Maradona had a disappointing World Cup in 1982, but certainly made up for it with his inspirational goals in Mexico four years later.

JOSEF MASOPUST – CZECHOSLOVAKIA

Josef was the only Czech to have been voted European Footballer of the Year, which he achieved in 1962 after a decade of being one of Central Europe's all-time greats. Born in Most on 9 February 1931, his international career began in 1954. He reached his peak in the World Cup in Chile in 1962, when inspiring Czechoslovakia's progress to the Final, and another highlight was scoring the opening goal against Brazil. After retiring, he became manager of the Czechoslovakian national team from 1984 until 1987.

BOBBY MOORE – ENGLAND

Bobby Moore completed a unique hat-trick when he climbed the Wembley steps as England's captain in 1966 to collect the World Cup after the dramatic 4–2 extra-time victory over West Germany. He had made the same triumph and ascent twice before in the previous two years as West Ham's skipper, first to lift the FA Cup in 1964, and second to pick up the European Cup Winners' Cup. Moore established a record number of international caps – 108 – was voted Player of the Tournament in 1966, and was again England's outstanding performer in Mexico in 1970.

GERD MULLER – WEST GERMANY

Nicknamed 'Der Bomber', Muller blitzed defences with more explosive results than any other striker in West German history. Including qualifying matches Muller scored 19 goals in the 1970 series, with 10 in the Finals; his contribution to West Germany's World Cup crown in 1974 was 4 goals, and he had a record Finals aggregate of 14. He was just as prolific with Bayern Munich, for whom he scored more than 600 goals in all competitions. Born in Bavaria on 3 November 1945, he began his career with his local club Nordlingen, and joined Bayern Munich in 1964 after several clubs had decided that he was too thick-set and stocky to be sufficiently mobile against top defences. His 36 goals in European Cup football made nonsense of that opinion. He had scored 68 goals in 62 matches for West Germany when he announced his retirement from international football, before exporting his goal-power to the United States of America.

DIETER MULLER – WEST GERMANY

Like his famous namesake, Gerd, Dieter was an attacker who liked to play at centre-forward, always searching for good openings to run into with speed. Dieter had his introduction to international football in the 1976 European Nations' Championship, when he scored against Yugoslavia with his first touch of the ball.

JOHANN NEESKENS – HOLLAND

Neeskens really shone in the 1974 World Cup, in particular by scoring many goals from penalties including one early on in the Final. He followed Cruyff to play in Spain and was a member of the Ajax of Amsterdam side which won the European Cup three years in succession in the early 1970s.

ANTON ONDRAUS – CZECHOSLOVAKIA

Tall, fair-haired centre-back Ondraus was absolutely authoritative in his country's victory in the 1976 European Nations' Championship. Not surprisingly for a tall man, his play with the head was superb, and he was also a very intelligent player. His good form was one of the reasons why his country went unbeaten through a period of two years from 1975.

SILVIO PIOLA – ITALY

The most prolific goal-scorer in Italian football history, Piola was the outstanding centre-forward in the 1938 Finals held in France. His two goals helped to lift Italy to their 4–2 victory over Hungary in the Final in Paris. Born in Robbio Romellina on 29 September 1913, he had a long and eventful career that included 32 international appearances. He scored twice on his debut for Italy against Austria in 1937, and made his final international appearance against England in Florence in 1952 at the age of thirty-eight. At the close of his playing career he became manager of the Italian Under-23 team. In February 1951 he finally notched the goal that beat Peppino Meazza's record aggregate Italian League haul of 355 goals.

PELÉ – BRAZIL

At his peak Pelé was a footballing phenomenon, widely acclaimed as the most accomplished all-round player in the world. His performances across the globe, whether for Santos Brazil or New York Cosmos, have been witnessed with an awe and appreciation unequalled in the history of the game. Born in 1940 in Tres Coracoes, Brazil, the son of a professional footballer, Pelé became known to his family as 'Dico', but his real name was Edson Arantes Di Nascimento. He was given the nickname 'Pelé' at school, a name which has no literal meaning in Portuguese. A natural athlete, he excelled at football and after many notable performances at junior level he joined the Santos club when he was fifteen. With Santos he scored the first of his career total of 1300 goals in a match against Corinthians on 7 September 1956. He confirmed his early promise with a goal on his debut for Brazil, and then contributed to a 2–1 win against Argentina the following year when he was seventeen years of age. In the yellow and green shirt of Brazil, Pelé became the scourge of international defences the world over, and he played in three World Cup Championships – in 1958, 1962 and 1970. Although he missed the 1962 Final through injury, he scored in each of the other two – twice against Sweden in 1958, and once against Italy in 1970. His former Brazilian team manager, Saldanha, once said of Pelé: 'If you asked me who was the best footballer in Brazil, I would say Pelé. If you asked me who was the best winger, I would say Pelé, and if you asked who was the best goalkeeper, I would have to say Pelé. He is like no other footballer.'

FRANTISEK PLANICKA – CZECHOSLOVAKIA

One of Europe's most accomplished goalkeepers before the war, Planicka kept Czechoslovakia in the 1934 World Cup Finals with a series of magnificent saves. Yet in the Final it was his failure to read a curling shot from Raymond Orsi that cost the Czechs any chance of holding Italy. Born in 1904, he played in 74 internationals for Czechoslovakia, and captained both his country and his club side, Slavia Prague, with whom he won eight League Championship medals between 1924 and 1937. He was again Czechoslovakia's last line of defence in the 1938 World Cup, breaking an arm in the bruising quarter-final match against Brazil.

MICHEL PLATINI – FRANCE

The best player in France next to the legendary Raymond Copa, always full of enthusiasm whether advancing from midfield or on the attack. He possessed abundant skill and a great deal of resolution. He seemed also to have the convenient habit of being at the right place at the right time to score goals. Sadly, under his managership of France the national team failed to qualify for this year's World Cup competition.

FERENC PUSKAS – HUNGARY

Born in Budapest in 1926, with his stunningly powerful left-foot shot and his ability to be a thought and deed ahead of most defenders, Puskas was probably the most influential player in the magnificent Hungarian team of the 1950s that went four years and 29 games without a single defeat. The unbeaten run sadly ended in the 1954 World Cup Final, when Puskas was still playing despite an ankle injury which robbed him of much of his fire and flair. After the 1956 Hungarian uprising, Puskas added to his reputation as one of the greatest players of all time by becoming a front-line master with Real Madrid, for whom he scored four goals in the 1960 European Cup Final. Puskas was often Hungarian captain, winning 84 national caps before his defection in 1956.

ALF RAMSEY – ENGLAND

Born in Dagenham on 22 January 1920, this former international full-back was knighted for masterminding England's 1966 World Cup triumph. He was such a calculating, tactically minded right-back that his team-mates in the famous push-and-run Tottenham team of the 1950s nicknamed him the 'General'. After playing 32 games for England, Ramsey retired in 1955 and switched, with tremendous success, to management with Ipswich Town, leading them from the Third Division to the Second and then the First Division Championships, a title double that he also achieved as a player with Spurs. Appointed as successor to England's team manager Walter Winterbottom in 1962, he brought a new era of professionalism to the English set-up. Ramsey burdened himself with the prophecy that England would win the World Cup in 1966, then came up with the tactics and the team which would make it come true. His full record as England's manager was: played 105, won 66, drawn 24, lost 14, goals for 213, goals against 90. He was sacked after England's failure to qualify for the 1974 World Cup Finals.

JONNY REP – HOLLAND

Rep's instinct for being in the right place at the right time, as well as his fierce finishing shot, made him an important linch-pin in the Ajax and Dutch teams of the 1970s. It was his headed goal that clinched a hat-trick of European Cup Finals for Ajax against Juventus in 1973. Rep contributed four goals in the 1974 World Cup Finals, and another three in 1978. Although lacking the skill of some of his team-mates, he could disturb the tightest defences with his power and drive. He later starred in French football, giving punch to the St Etienne attack.

ROBERTO RIVELINO – BRAZIL

Rivelino came on to the international scene in 1968, when he toured with the Brazilian team. He played in the 1970 and 1974 World Cups, showing many talents and a sharpness at dead-ball situations. He used his greatest skills – of passing the ball accurately together with his thunderous shooting – to pose threats to all defences.

DOMINIQUE ROCHETEAU – FRANCE

No one will forget the eight minutes Rocheteau played for St Etienne in the European Cup Final of 1976, when there was hardly enough time to demonstrate all his amazing skills with the ball, in both wonderful dribbling and fierce shooting. He played in attack for France, and gave pleasure to very many with his incisive play.

KARL HEINZ RUMMENIGGE – WEST GERMANY

An attacker of great flair, he burst on to the scene during the 1975–76 season, and played for Bayern Munich when the club won the European Cup for the third successive time. He was inclined to be over-enthusiastic, almost to the point of being rather selfish.

NILTON SANTOS – BRAZIL

His sixteen appearances in World Cup Final matches constitute a record for Brazil. In 1962 he became, at thirty-six, the oldest man to collect a World Cup winner's medal, and he was still determined enough to win his 85th cap at the age of forty. He was a skilful and composed left-back who balanced perfectly with his long-term partner, Djalma Santos. Both of them were masters of positive, overlapping play, and used to take turns to make probing runs into opposition territory. Born near Rio de Janeiro in 1926, Nilton had a long career with Botafogo. He was noted for his coolness and command in moments of crisis, a reputation which was dented in the notorious 'Battle of Berne', when he was sent off. A World Cup winner in 1958 and 1962.

UWE SEELER – WEST GERMANY

No one has played more matches in World Cup Final tournaments than Seeler, who between 1958 and 1970 appeared in 21 games for West Germany. He skippered the West German team that finished runners-up to England in 1966, and was also an influential player for the Germans in 1958, 1962 and 1970. Though short and stocky, he was an acrobatic centre-forward who could outjump even the tallest defence to score with flying headers. Seeler was courageous and fought off several injury handicaps to remain in international football for a span of 72 matches. Born in Hamburg in 1936, he served SV Hamburg as a prolific goal-scorer for twenty years. He was leading marksman in the West German League on five occasions, and played his first match for West Germany at the age of seventeen. His World Cup career seemed to be over after he had inspired his country to the runners-up position in 1966, but he made a comeback to the international arena in 1970 and, concentrating on an auxiliary attacking role, gave Gerd Muller sufficient support to lift the Germans into third position in the tournament.

NOBBY STILES – ENGLAND

Born in Manchester on 18 May 1942, this warrior of a footballer was totally committed to every match he played in and was rarely popular with the opposition, who felt the fierce force of his challenges. He was a midfield motivator of the England team that won the 1966 World Cup, and also for the Manchester United team that won the European Cup in 1968. Although small and slight, he strolled the pitch like a giant and was frightened of no situation or reputation. He was a master of winning the ball with well-timed interception and biting tackles. It was thanks to his dynamic approach to every game that the teams he played with would enjoy so much possession. He would win the ball and then pass it to players with greater shooting skills to capitalise on his work. Despite wearing contact lenses for playing, he had a good eye for turning defence into attack with well-delivered passes.

MARIO TARDELLI – ITALY

Tardelli usually played full-back for his country and midfield for his club, Juventus. First capped in April 1976, his powerful running forward and deceptive change of pace helped to set up scoring chances for his colleagues.

BILLY WRIGHT – ENGLAND

This stalwart defender captained England in the World Cup Finals of 1954 and 1958. He was a magnificent field-marshal, captaining Wolves to a succession of memorable triumphs in the 1950s and leading England 90 times, while winning the then record of 105 international caps. Born at Ironbridge, Shropshire on 6 February 1924, he began his career as an inside-forward, later developing into a driving right-half. He switched to centre-half in an emergency for the 1954 World Cup Finals, and went on to establish himself as one of England's greatest ever central defenders, greatly respected by team-mates and opponents alike. He is now a successful television executive.

LEV YASHIN – RUSSIA

One of the legendary figures of football, Yashin was Russia's commanding last line of defence in 74 international matches, during which he became world renowned for his ability and astounding reflex saves. Born in Moscow in 1929, he played throughout his career for Moscow Dynamos. His loyalty to the club was rewarded in 1971 when a capacity 100,000 crowd packed the Lenin Stadium to see Yashin in his farewell match, skippering a Moscow Dynamos team against a Rest of the World side captained by Bobby Charlton. Standing 6 feet 2 inches and always dressed in black, he was an imposing figure on the goal-line, and his expert positioning and apparently telescopic reach meant that forwards were rarely given more than a glimpse of their target. He played for Russia in the World Cup Finals of 1958, 1962 and 1966, and travelled to Mexico in 1970 as a distinguished reserve.

ZICO – BRAZIL

A midfield player of great skill, he had a very wide vision of the pitch. Zico liked to make passes of up to 40 metres, and was always running forward to score goals. In fact, in 1974 he finished the season as Brazil's top scorer, and people thought he would be another Tostao – but perhaps another Garrincha, with his magic dribbling, is a more appropriate description.

DINO ZOFF – ITALY

Following Gordon Banks' retirement, Zoff challenged Sepp Maier for the title of the world's greatest goalkeeper. Born on 28 February 1942, tall and agile and with excellent positional sense and reflexes, he made appearances in the winning side for the 1968 European Nations' Championships and in the 1974 and other World Cup sides. When Haiti scored against Italy in the 1974 World Cup Finals, it was the first time in 1143 minutes of international football that Zoff had been beaten. Zoff joined Juventus from Naples in 1972, and captained the 1978 Italian team in Argentina.

WOULD YOU BELIEVE?

The United States trainer raced on to the pitch to protest to the referee over a disputed decision during the 1930 semi-final against Argentina. He stumbled and dropped his box of medical supplies, including a bottle of chloroform which smashed on the pitch. The trainer took the fumes full in the face as he bent to pick up the box. He folded slowly to the ground and had to be carried back to the touch-line bench!

?

Ten chartered boats spilling over with Argentinian supporters sailed across the River Plate to Montevideo in 1930. Only the first two to sail docked in time for the Final – the other eight were delayed by thick fog. Match referee John Langenus was aboard the first of the boats.

Hector Castro, scorer of Uruguay's victory-clinching fourth goal in the 1930 Final, had only one hand. He had lost his right hand and part of his arm in a childhood accident.

?

Argentinian-born Raimondo Orsi scored a spectacular goal for Italy against Czechoslovakia in the 1934 Final, his right-foot shot sending the ball on a curling trail into the net. The day after the Final, Orsi tried more than twenty times to repeat the shot for the benefit of a posse of photographers. He failed.

?

Leonidas da Silva, flamboyant star of Brazil's 1938 attack, was unhappy playing against Poland on the muddy pitch at Strasbourg. He decided he would have better grip if he played barefoot. However, the moment he removed his boots and tossed them over the touch-line, the referee ordered him to put them back on because it was in contravention of the laws of the game to play without boots. The game was held up while Leonidas replaced his boots and went on to score four goals in a remarkable 6–5 victory. Ernest Willimowski scored four goals for Poland and still finished on the losing side.

Dr Charles Dietz, Hungary's sole selector for the 1938 Finals, said before the Hungarians played Switzerland in their quarter-finals match at Lille: 'If we don't beat the Swiss, I'll walk home to Hungary.' Dr Georges Sarosi, the Hungarian centre-forward, captain and a lawyer by profession, overheard and insisted that Dr Dietz put his statement in writing. There were several frights for Dr Dietz before Hungary finally mastered the Swiss 2–0.

?

Italian skipper Guiseppe Meazza had that sinking feeling as he scored the semi-final penalty against Brazil that clinched a place in the 1938 Final. As he steered the spot-kick into the net his shorts, torn earlier in the game, slipped down to leave him exposed. His celebrating team-mates hid his blushes until a new pair was produced.

?

With war clouds gathering over Europe, Jules Rimet – then President of FIFA and the man after whom the World Cup trophy was named – reclaimed the trophy from the Italian FA. He thought long and hard about where it would be safest, eventually deciding that the only place was his bedroom where it nestled for the whole of the Second World War.

Yugoslav inside-left Rajko Mitic walked into an iron girder as he was leaving the dressing room for the start of the 1950 match against Brazil at the Maracana Stadium, gashing his forehead and knocking himself out. The ten remaining players went out on to the pitch for the pre-match ceremony and then started to walk back to the dressing room in a bid to delay the kick-off. Welsh referee Mervyn Griffiths insisted they start the game straight away, and so Brazil kicked off against ten men. By the time the heavily bandaged and still dazed Mitic joined the action, Yugoslavia were a goal down and they were finally beaten 2–0. Later in his career, Mitic became manager of the Yugoslav national team.

?

Skipper Danny Blanchflower told startled reporters that Northern Ireland's secret tactic was always 'to equalise before the opposition scores'. The Irish have a party after every match, win, lose or draw. An 'outsider' walked into a swinging party after Northern Ireland had been beaten 3–1 by Argentina. 'What are you celebrating?' he asked manager Peter Doherty. 'We're drowning our sorrows,' he replied with a wide grin. The Irish laughed all the way into the quarter-finals.

?

The biggest crowd the Argentinian players faced in 1958 was the one waiting for them at the airport in Buenos Aires on their arrival home. Thousands gathered at the airport to greet them with a shower of rotten tomatoes, stones and fruit, in a show of disgust at their performances in the Finals where they had been beaten 3–1 by West Germany and 6–1 by Czechoslovakia. A mob also descended on the Argentinian FA headquarters, smashing windows and tearing up fencing.

Pelé was so pleased with the two-goal debut of his deputy, Amarildo, for Brazil against Spain in 1962 that he jumped, fully clothed, into the team bath after the match to congratulate him!

?

In 1966 the World Cup had its first four-legged hero. The Jules Rimet Trophy was stolen while on exhibition at a stamp show in Central Hall, Westminster. There was a massive police hunt for the missing trophy and, just when it looked as if football's number one prize had disappeared completely, it was unearthed by a dog called Pickles, who sniffed it out from its hiding place under a bush in Norwood, south London. Pickles and his owner collected a £6000 reward and a man who had demanded a £15,000 ransom for the return of the trophy was jailed for two years.

?

Alan Ball was so bitterly disappointed by England's 3–2 defeat by West Germany in the 1970 quarter-finals that he threw his tournament medal out of his hotel bedroom window.

Tostao gave his Brazilian shirt and his World Cup winner's medal to the surgeon in Houston, Texas who had performed two operations on a detached retina in his eye in the year immediately preceding the 1970 Finals.

?

The West Germans staged a spectacular opening ceremony to the 1974 Finals which involved meticulous organisation. But they had overlooked one minor detail. As Brazil and Yugoslavia lined up for the kick-off to the opening match in the stadium at Frankfurt, the referee delayed the start while embarrassed officials hustled around the pitch putting in the corner and centre-line flags.

THE QUALIFYING COUNTRIES

Argentina	Republic of Ireland
Austria	Romania
Belgium	Scotland
Brazil	South Korea
Cameroon	Spain
Columbia	Sweden
Costa Rica	United Arab Emirates
Czechoslovakia	United States of America
Egypt	Uruguay
England	USSR
Holland	West Germany
Italy	Yugoslavia

(We suggest you fill in the colours on the national flags.)

ARGENTINA

Capital Buenos Aires
Population 31 million

Football was introduced here by British residents of Buenos Aires at the end of the last century, but it wasn't until the arrival of Italian immigrants early in this century that the game took hold of the public's imagination. During the 1930s and 1950s, wealthy Italian clubs raided the football market in Argentina and carried off many great players.

In more recent times, many exceptional world-class players of local fame have been sold to Italian and Spanish clubs, Alfredo Di Stefano, Mario Kempes and Diego Maradona to name but three. Traditionally skilful and pleasing, local football deprived of such star players has often resulted in a crude and over-physical style of play. The top clubs in the country are Boca Juniors, River Plate and Independiente. Whereas River Plate are seen as the wealthy set-up, Boca are the Italian club from the port, founded in 1913 by an Irishman, Patrick MacCarthy, and a group of newly arrived Italian immigrants. They won the South American Club Cup Final in 1977 and 1978. Great rivals River Plate won that competition in 1986, then went one better by overcoming Steaua of Romania for the world crown. Independiente landed the South American title in 1972 and the World Club title in 1973, beating Juventus 1–0 in Rome, and again in 1984 against Liverpool, also 1–0, in Tokyo. Midfielder Ricardo Bochini has been their most recent well-known player.

Argentina was producing great players in the 1920s, including Ferreyra, but it took them until 1978 to win the World Cup. The triumphant host–manager was charismatic Cesar Menotti, who had been succeeded by Carlos Bilado when they repeated the achievement in Mexico in 1986.

The world champions were disappointed in the 1989 South American Championship after having received poor service from their foreign-based stars Maradona and Burrachaga, who had made such a difference to the team when they had won the previous World Cup. Goalkeeper Pumpido and striker Caniggia were the only players worthy of a mention in the South American tournament. They scored only two goals in the seven matches of the tournament, failing to beat the likes of Ecuador and Bolivia. Manager Carlos Bilado was not helped by the physical and mental fatigue of Maradona, back from Italy, nor by all the transfer speculation surrounding his captain. In the end it wore the player down so much that he locked himself in his hotel room! Despite all this, Maradona produced the most imaginative moment of the whole tournament when he struck the Uruguayan bar from inside the centre circle. Also on the positive side, youngsters Sensini, Basualdo, Troglio and Caniggia showed that they have bright international futures.

The manager's main concern before the World Cup will be to strengthen the attack, possibly by bringing back Gabriel Calderon, Dezotti, Diaz or Dertytia, most of whom are gaining valuable experience abroad. Bilado says: 'I think that the squad can do itself justice in Italy as long as they don't come to me tired and with injury problems. If only I could have two full months with them beforehand, that would be magnificent.'

Player to watch: Maradona – who else?

AUSTRIA

Capital Vienna
Population 8 million

Austria played a leading part in international soccer throughout the first half of this century. The 'Viennese' style of play was artistic, skilled and based on short passing. Influential in this successful period was Hugo Meisl and his chief coach from Britain, Jimmy Hogan.

Austria took fourth place in the 1934 Finals but by the time of the 1954 World Cup had passed their peak, although they did reach the semi-final, only to be beaten by West Germany 6–1.

Austria reached the second stage of both the 1978 and 1982 World Cup Finals – a solid achievement for a small nation.

Domestic soccer has, in the meantime, slumped, with average gates around 4000 – although recent European successes may reverse the trend. When national team manager Branko Elsner resigned in 1987 he warned: 'We are third rate – I can see no future for Austrian football!'

Will he be proved wrong?

Player to watch: Polster, a prolific scorer.

BELGIUM

Capital Brussels
Population 10 million

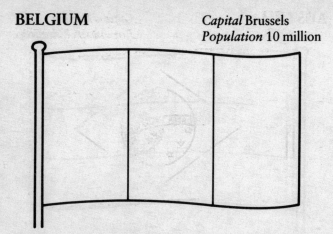

In earlier times Belgium staged and won the 1920 Olympics, and later were one of only four teams to travel to Uruguay for the first World Cup. It is only quite recently, however, that they have re-emerged as a force in international football. That period began with Anderlecht contesting the 1970 Fairs Cup Final against Arsenal. While the national team took third place in the 1972 European Championship, Belgium also qualified for the 1982 and 1986 World Cup competitions, taking fourth place in the latter, an indication of the progress made during the last decade. Jan Ceulemans, as captain, was largely responsible for holding the young side together in Mexico.

Player to watch: Ceulemans, an experienced general.

BRAZIL

Capital Brasilia
Population 138 million

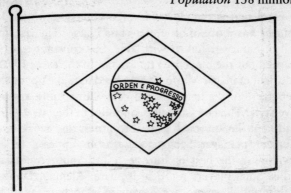

Introduced by Britain, football in Brazil was truly
developed by a Hungarian, Dori Kurschner, who put
across the idea of team-work and tactics to add to
natural flair. Go to Brazil and at any time you will see on
the famous Copa Cobana beach outside Rio de Janeiro
thousands of youngsters playing for hour after hour
under the hot sun, and nearby a group of pitches where
they play enthusiastically all through the night. Not
surprisingly, therefore, Brazil is a country that has
consistently produced an army of magnificently talented
players, ball jugglers of genius and intuitive in their
grasp of how the game should be played.

Brazil was the first nation to win the World Cup three
times, and also the first to win in a different continent. It
also gave the game Pelé. It is of no surprise, therefore,
that despite limited international success over the past
two decades, the name Brazil is still synonymous with
the skill, excitement and magic of the World Cup. Their
pulling power is still supreme because they have a
history of producing great players, many of whom have
broken through racial and poverty barriers to become

rich and famous; Pelé, Didì and Garrincha are but three of these.

Flamengo is the club side of the masses, while Fluminese has more of an upper-class image. The rise and fall of Santos is linked with Pelé, but constant touring burned out the players of that team. In the early 1970s, national manager Mario Zagalo tried to make up for the departure of the inspirational Pelé with a more aggressive style. The late Claudio Coutinho, in the late 1970s, had kept the approach geared to fitness and work-rate. Current manager Sebastiao Lazaroni appears to be combining the best of European and South American skills. Such players as Ricardo, Tita, Alemao, Dunga, Valdo and Romario are Brazilians who have adapted their gifts successfully to European football.

In 1989 Brazil celebrated their first major success since the World Cup of 1970 when they won the South American Championship before a 115,000 crowd in Rio's Maracana Stadium. A goal by Romario provided a 1–0 victory over Uruguay. In fact, it was exactly 39 years ago that Brazil lost 2–1 in the World Cup Finals to Uruguay at the same venue. Coach Sebastiao Lazaroni's workmanlike tactics were justified; he has always said that he is not interested in playing 'pretty' soccer but only in getting results. Taffarel looked like the best goalkeeper Brazil have had for a long time, and Bebeto finally confirmed the brilliant talent he has suggested over the years. Remember, too, that this was a Brazil deprived by injury of Careca and Tita, and with Muller unavailable because of Turin's fight against relegation.

International football undoubtedly needs a successful Brazil, because the nation epitomises entertainment, excitement and skill.

Player to watch: Careca, who may regain his form dramatically.

CAMEROON

Capital Yaoundé
Population 9 million

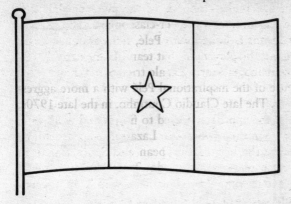

Cameroon was the first black African nation to make an impact in international football, appearing in the 1982 World Cup Finals, so far their only appearance to date. They forced draws with Italy, Poland and Peru, statistics which give them the record of never having lost a World Cup Finals match!

The team beat Tunisia 2–0 at home and 1–0 away to reach the Finals. Goalkeeper Thomas Nkono, African Footballer of the Year, has also starred in Spain with Espanol. Cameroon are current African champions having been runners-up to Egypt, the hosts, in 1986.

Player to watch: Oman Biyjck, a new black star.

AMAZING FACT

No fewer than 18 of the 55 different finalists failed to win a match, but only one of them has yet to be defeated. Cameroon drew all three of their 1982 matches, but were still eliminated.

COLUMBIA

Capital Bogotá
Population 25 million

Columbia topped group two of the South American groups and qualified by beating Israel, the Oceania winners, in a play-off.

Columbia made their only previous appearance in the Finals in Chile in 1962, drawing one of their games and losing the other two. Although traditionally the 'Cinderella' of South American soccer, Columbia can afford to pay top rates and take major stars from Argentina, Brazil and Uruguay for their domestic football teams.

Player to watch: Valderrama, 1987 Footballer of the Year in South America.

COSTA RICA

Capital San José
Population 3 million

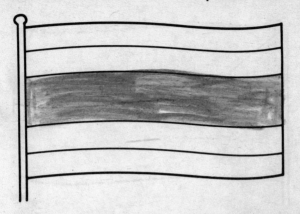

Making their first appearance in a World Cup, Costa Rica qualified with the United States in the North/Central American group. They are an unknown quantity, Mexico having dominated Central America since international football has been played there. With Mexico banned from international football until the end of 1990, it is now up to smaller neighbours Costa Rica to fly the flag for Central America.

Player to watch: Flores, star striker.

CZECHOSLOVAKIA

Capital Prague
Population 16 million

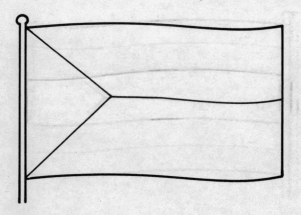

Czechoslovakian football has a long tradition dating back to the last century, even before the country existed! The Bohemian city of Prague was long an established footballing capital of Central Europe. Czechoslovakia reached the 1934 World Cup Finals and led hosts Italy with nine minutes to go, but eventually lost 2–1 in extra time. As in all Eastern Bloc countries, the army sports section became a focal point for football achievement. It was around the core of Dukla Prague's fine side that the national team was built, the side which finished runners-up to Brazil in the 1962 World Cup. Czechoslovakia have, however, faded somewhat from the international scene since they won the European Championship in 1976.

Player to watch: Michael Bilek, a dynamic midfielder who takes a mean free-kick.

EGYPT

Capital Cairo
Population 51 million

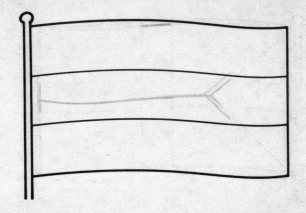

Although a major force in African football, this will be their first appearance in the World Cup Finals since 1934. They have won the African Cup on three occasions, most recently, in 1986, in front of a 100,000 crowd in Cairo, the home of the African Confederation.

Egypt join Cameroon as Africa's representatives, having beaten Algeria 1–0 in the final stage of the qualifying competition.

Player to watch: It could be anybody – Taher Abu-Zeid is the Maradona of Egypt.

ENGLAND

Capital London
Population 46 million

The Football Association was founded in 1863, and the FA Cup introduced in 1871. With regard to international football, England withdrew from FIFA in 1928 after having made a protest about the professionalism that seemed widespread within the officially amateur Olympic tournaments. They remained outside FIFA until 1946, having refused an offer to compete in the tournament Finals in 1938 in France.

The characteristics of the English game are its great vigour and professionalism, qualities appreciated by Alf Ramsey in taking the team to World Cup victory in 1966. Later knighted for his achievements, Sir Alf's 'Wingless Wonders' had overcome some uninspiring early matches to win a marvellous and gripping Final 4–2 against West Germany. The emergence of Gary Lineker and Peter Beardsley in 1986 took them to the quarter-finals and a controversial defeat by Argentina. England's campaign in the European Championships Finals in 1988 was a major disappointment. Defeats by the Republic of Ireland, Holland and the Soviet Union left them bottom of their group. However, England can never be written off as an international force. Although other countries have caught up in terms of players and tactics, English football is still highly regarded throughout the world.

Player to watch: Robson, the complete player.

HOLLAND

Capital Amsterdam
Population 15 million

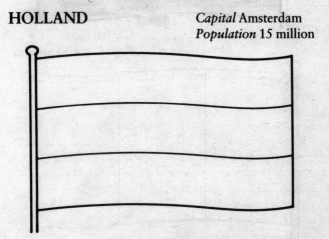

Holland had no team in the World Cup Finals tournaments between 1938 and 1974, which is a strange statistic about Dutch football. Soccer appeared on the Dutch scene at the beginning of the century under the influence of British coaches, but professionalism was a long time in coming. Since the war there have been two distinct periods: up to 1956, when regional leagues were played using amateur players; and since that date, when the league has been dominated by Ajax of Amsterdam and Feyenoord of Rotterdam, both of whom have won the European Cup, the former on three successive occasions.

In Johann Cruyff and Johann Neeskens, Holland possessed players of high quality. Failure to qualify for the Finals in 1982 and 1986 meant a lean period from which the new European Championship team, including Ruud Gullit and Marco van Basten, has emerged to renew Dutch spirits and expectations for 1990.

Player to watch: Gullit, who may be more influential than Maradona.

ITALY

Capital Rome
Population 58 million

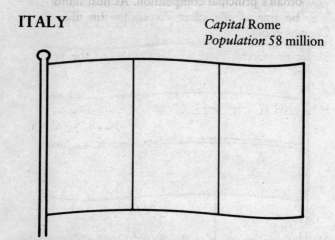

Although the game was introduced to Italy by a Turin businessman, Eduardo Bosio, it was in England that he had first been taken by the game. Genoa Football and Cricket Club was the first of the great Italian clubs, and English entrepreneurs had much to do with it. A key figure in the early years of the game in Italy, however, was undoubtedly Vittorio Pozzo, who was in charge of the Italian team which played in the 1912 Olympics in Stockholm, and who managed the professional team from 1929 to 1948, twice winning the World Cup. Since the war the amount of paper money attached to the game has grown rapidly, and transfer fees paid for players have expanded out of all proportion. Year in and year out the same four teams from Milan, Turin (AC Milan and Internazionale of Turin), Juventus and Torino finish in the top places. Tactically shrewd, the Italian players are fiercely drilled and are formidable World Cup opponents. Victory in the 1982 World Cup Final enabled Italy to match Brazil's record of three wins in football's principal competition. As host nation they will be one of the clear favourites for this year's Championship.

Player to watch: Vialli, the sensation of the year in Europe.

REPUBLIC OF IRELAND   *Capital* Dublin
Population 4 million

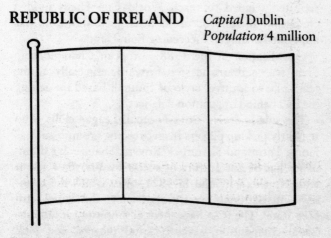

Eire national teams used to be picked by selection committees until the appointment in 1969 of Mike Meegan, who became the first manager to be accorded full rights of team selection. He kept the job for three years, to be succeeded by ex-Newcastle United player Liam Tuohy, one of whose first acts was to take the team to the mini-World Cup Final held in Brazil in 1972. He returned with two wins and the feeling that there were the makings of a good side. Tuohy was succeeded in turn by the man who did so much to bring that scheme to fruition, Johnny Giles, a very gifted midfield player with Leeds United. Giles had won his first cap at the age of eighteen when with Manchester United, and now holds the record number of caps. His first game as manager of the Republic was in November 1973 against the Polish team that had just put England out of the 1974 World Cup by holding them to a 1–1 draw. The Irish won their game 1–0, and from then on Giles thought the best way to run a team from a small country was like a club side. However, the country repeatedly failed to reach World Cup Finals until a change in fortune occurred after Jack Charlton was appointed manager, succeeding Eoin Hand.

Qualification in the 1988 European Championship Final was a dramatic step forward, especially as the team played a direct style of football based on getting the ball behind opposition defences.

The side is drawn from Football League clubs, who regularly pick up players from breeding grounds such as Home Farm and Shamrock Rovers. Shamrock's dominance has been a feature of soccer history since a split with Northern Ireland in 1921, after which the country's internationals were played under the name 'Irish Free State'. The Irish have great enthusiasm for international competition, several skilful players, and Jack Charlton's management and coaching qualities – all important ingredients for a successful World Cup campaign.

Player to watch: Whelan, who may reproduce his Liverpool form.

ROMANIA

Capital Bucharest
Population 23 million

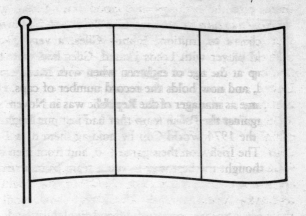

Romania earned their place in footballing history when King Carol II agreed to pay the wages and expenses of the top players while they travelled to Uruguay for the first World Cup Finals in 1930. They also appeared in 1934 and 1938, returning in 1970. British engineers in the Ploesti oilfield had originally taken the game to Romania at the turn of the century. The Romanians have until recently lived in the shadow of their more famous East European neighbours, but their progress at club level was confirmed in 1986 by Steaua Bucharest in a victory over Barcelona in the European Cup Final. The team then proved that the win had been no fluke by defeating Kiev in the Super Cup. Centre-forward Robion Camatutaru scored 44 goals in 1987 to earn the Golden Boot as Europe's top league scorer.

Player to watch: Itagi, an exciting player hoping to make a big impact.

SCOTLAND

Capital Edinburgh
Population 7 million

In the early days the country followed England's lead, with Queen's Park, the leading Scottish club of the time, also a member of the English Football Association. The same club, however, was responsible for setting up the Scottish FA and a Scottish competition in 1873.

Like England, Scotland refused to enter the first World Cup Finals, not taking part until after the Second World War. This was a pity in view of the abundance of talent around in the 1930s such as Hughie Gallagher, Alex James and Alan Morton.

Scotland have been disappointing in the sense that they have qualified for five successive Final tournaments, but have never yet progressed beyond the first-round stage of the Finals.

For the 1990 campaign manager Andy Roxburgh is faced with the considerable task of breaking the national capacity for self-delusion. Most Scotsmen may believe their team will win the World Cup, but most non-Scots think that highly unlikely. Roxburgh explains, 'Outsiders don't know quite what to make of us. More often than not we don't know what to make of ourselves.' Time will tell.

Player to watch: Jim Leighton, prone to goalkeeping errors, but good performances from him will lift the Scots.

SOUTH KOREA

Capital Seoul
Population 43 million

South Korea have made two appearances in the competition, in 1954 and 1986. They were always expected to top the World Cup Asian qualifying group 4, but the extent of their superiority surprised many people. With the advantage of staging the first half of the tournament in Seoul, they put together a played 6, won 6 record, scoring 25 goals without conceding one. In the second stage of qualification in Singapore they held off the challenge of five other nations including the powerful Chinese team.

Player to watch: Choi Soon Ho, a regular goal scorer.

SPAIN

Capital Madrid
Population 39 million

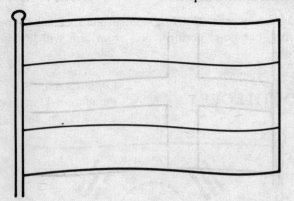

Despite boasting big clubs like Real Madrid and Barcelona, who are regular contenders for major European honours, Spain has seldom been able to produce an outstanding national team. Their best World Cup performance was to finish fourth in 1950. After a poor 1982 performance, the worst by any host country, 1986 represented an improvement, with a quarter-final defeat by Belgium on penalties. Along the way they met Denmark in a second-round tie and Emilo Butragueno scored four goals in the 5–1 victory over the Danes, the greatest individual scoring feat in a World Cup tournament since Eusebio's four against North Korea twenty years earlier. 'El Buitre' – 'The Vulture' – was the nickname given to the goal-scoring hero of Real Madrid.

Player to watch: Butragueno, capable of turning any match.

SWEDEN

Capital Stockholm
Population 8 million

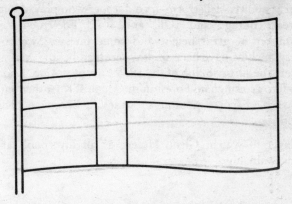

Sweden was one of the first continental countries to adopt soccer as a national game. Like their Scandinavian neighbours Denmark, they have one of the oldest league championships dating back, in their case, to 1896. As early as 1908, the Swedes entered a team for the Olympic Games. Sweden competed in the World Cups of both 1934 and 1938, and since the war have gained their most outstanding achievement by finishing as runners-up to Brazil when hosting the 1958 World Cup Finals. In 1948 they won the Olympic Soccer Tournament, and after they had finished the final pool of the 1950 tournament, Italian clubs reached for their chequebooks. Of those who went to play in Italy, the most illustrious were the three Nordahl brothers, Gunner Gren, Nils Liedholm and Kurre Hamrin, an outside-right of verve and darting skills.

It was a small Yorkshireman, George Raynor, who began the process of making Sweden a powerful footballing nation in the years just after the war, and the systems he began to teach seemed to have laid the foundations for a healthy future, with the development of good players including Kindvall, a central striker of great ability, Hellstroem, a goalkeeper who played with great courage and skill, and Rald Edestroem, an attacker of great height and some finesse. Sweden's league clubs have been improving steadily, and Malmö were the surprise club of the 1979 European Cup, losing 1–0 to Nottingham Forest in the Final. IFK Gothenburg have also scored notable successes in European competition.

Player to watch: Glenn Hysen, as all Liverpool fans know already.

UNITED ARAB EMIRATES

Capital Abu Dhabi
Population 2 million

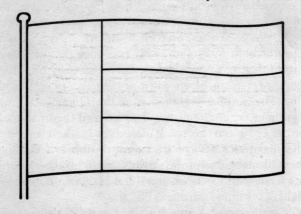

Little is known about the United Arab Emirates, one of the major surprise qualifiers for the 1990 World Cup Finals.

Their record in the qualifying rounds was good, including a notable victory against the strongly fancied Chinese. It is rumoured that the players were given a share of a £100,000 pool for reaching the Finals. Will this be sufficient motivation in Italy?

Player to watch: Adnan Khanis Talyani – known as Adnan and scorer of their winner against the Chinese.

UNITED STATES OF AMERICA

Capital Washington D.C.
Population 240 million

The United States became the twenty-fourth and final team to qualify, beating Trinidad and Tobago 1–0 before a boisterous overflow crowd of 35,000 in Port of Spain.

They have qualified twice for previous World Cup Finals, the first time in 1930 when they reached the semi-finals with a team which included five former Scottish professionals. On the second appearance in

1950 they gained a shock 1–0 victory over England, but that success was not built upon. During the 1960s, serious attempts were made to establish soccer internationally, culminating in the North American League. New York Cosmos even brought Pelé out of retirement to partner one of their best home-grown talents, Rick Davis. The experiment ultimately failed, and the national team have continued to be unsuccessful in their attempts to reach the World Cup Finals.

The situation is changing, however, with the United States qualifying in 1994 by virtue of guaranteed entry as hosts of the World Cup Competition.

Player to watch: the Californian Paul Caliguiri whose spectacular dipping shot secured America's place in the Finals.

URUGUAY

Capital Montevideo
Population 3 million

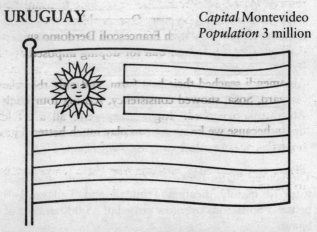

Ondino Viera, Uruguay's 1966 World Cup manager, summed up this tiny nation's remarkable record when he said: 'Other countries have their history; Uruguay has its football.'

They had become the first non-European Olympic champions in 1924, won the first World Cup in 1930 and, springing one of the game's biggest ever surprises in 1950, they beat run-away favourites Brazil in Rio de Janeiro to regain the World Cup. The Penarol and Nacionale clubs were in the forefront of launching the South American Club Cup. Great names over the years have included Obdlieo Barela, Rodriguez Andrede and Fernando Morena.

Although they lost the 100th American Championship to Brazil last year, the team look strong contenders. In Sosa they have an outstanding striker, and with the strong defence (not as physical as in the past), due in large part to the majestic Deleon and acrobatic Zeoli, they always seem to do just enough to come out on top and give the impression that they have something in reserve. During the South American Championship they were inconsistent, however. One problem was beginning the tournament with Francescoli Derdomo suspended; another a two-year ban for doping imposed upon Pablo Bengoechea. Neither Francescoli, Paz nor Alzamendi reached their best form, and only the other forward, Sosa, showed consistency, scoring four goals. Alzamendi remarked: 'Right now, we're all a bit let down because we know we can play much better. I just hope this doesn't affect us in the World Cup.'

Player to watch: Sosa, with the true Latin temperament to match his flair.

USSR

Capital Moscow
Population 281 million

Ever since the Soviets entered into international competition at the 1952 Olympics at Helsinki, they have been successful. They won the 1956 Olympics and the first ever European Nations' Championship four years later.

The English Charnock brothers introduced football to workers in the cotton mills in the 1880s. However, it was only when clubs such as Kiev Dynamo, from the Ukraine, and Tbelisi broke the Moscow domination that Soviet football began to make an impression on the world scene. Moscow Dynamo, however, remain an international legend because of their successful tour of Britain in 1945–46, before the Soviet Union had entered FIFA. Kiev Dynamo were the first to win a European trophy, the Cup Winners' Cup in 1975, thrilling spectators with their skill and technique.

Player to watch: Zavarov, an exciting player on the big occasion.

WEST GERMANY

Capital Bonn
Population 61 million

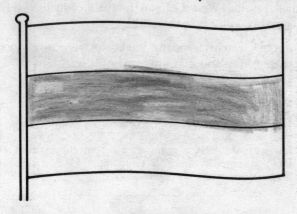

Football began here in the universities at the end of the last century and was much encouraged by local businessmen. The Association was founded in 1900, the game grew quickly and by the time the World Cup competition began, the team from Germany was a force very much to be reckoned with.

The fortunes of the national team had faded by the outbreak of the Second World War, however, with Germany outshone by many of the European nations. There was no national league in West Germany before 1963, the year in which the Bundeslega was formed – a move which undoubtedly improved the quality of the club sides. Bayern Munich and Borussia Münchengladbach were outstanding in the 1970s. It has been since the war, however, that the West German national team has been most impressive. Under the wily manager Sep Herberger, the team from West Germany won the World Cup in 1954. Under Helmut Schoen, who had served under Herberger for some time, came further triumphs, notably the 1974 World Cup and the 1972 European Nations' Championship. In terms of international results, West German football compares very favourably with any in the world.

Player to watch: So many quality players to choose from, but Matthaus may prove to be the star.

┌─ AMAZING FACT ──────────────────────────────┐

Sepp Maier (West Germany) conceded a goal to Holland in the first minute of the 1974 World Cup Final, but was not beaten again in the competition until Holland scored in the 1978 tournament. He had kept his goal intact for 475 minutes.

└──┘

YUGOSLAVIA

Capital Belgrade
Population 23 million

This country has been one of the greatest exporters of both coaching and playing talent. Even in 1930, when Yugoslavia were one of four European nations to attend the first World Cup in Uruguay, goal-scoring forward Ivan Bek was on his way to playing club soccer in France. Their record in the World Cup to date suggests that they have made a habit of being second-best, one reason perhaps being that National Service takes players out of the game at a crucial stage in their careers. There is a question mark over whether the Yugoslav team, which won the World Youth Cup in 1987, will fulfil its potential.

Player to watch: Susic, a player much admired by other professionals.

HOW THEY GOT TO ITALY

Europe

Winners and runners-up from groups 3, 5, 6 and 7 qualify for the finals along with the winners of groups 1, 2 and 4 plus the two runners-up from groups 1, 2 and 4 with the best comparative records.

Group 1

	P	W	D	L	F	A	Pts
Romania	6	4	1	1	10	5	9
Denmark	6	3	2	1	15	6	8
Greece	6	1	2	3	3	15	4
Bulgaria	6	1	1	4	6	8	3

ROMANIA qualify for the finals.

Group 2

	P	W	D	L	F	A	Pts
Sweden	6	4	2	0	9	3	10
England	6	3	3	0	10	0	9
Poland	6	2	1	3	4	8	5
Albania	6	0	0	6	3	15	0

SWEDEN, ENGLAND qualify for the finals.

Group 3

	P	W	D	L	F	A	Pts
Soviet Union	8	4	3	1	11	4	11
Austria	8	3	3	2	9	9	9
Turkey	8	3	1	4	12	10	7
East Germany	8	3	1	4	9	13	7
Iceland	6	1	4	3	6	11	6

SOVIET UNION, AUSTRIA qualify for the finals.

Group 4

	P	W	D	L	F	A	Pts
Holland	6	4	2	0	8	2	10
West Germany	6	3	3	0	13	3	9
Finland	6	1	1	4	4	16	3
Wales	6	0	2	4	4	8	2

HOLLAND, WEST GERMANY qualify for the finals.

Group 5

	P	W	D	L	F	A	Pts
Yugoslavia	8	6	2	0	16	6	14
Scotland	8	4	2	2	12	12	10
France	8	3	3	2	10	7	9
Norway	8	2	2	4	10	9	6
Cyprus	8	0	1	7	6	20	1

YUGOSLAVIA, SCOTLAND qualify for the finals.

Group 6

	P	W	D	L	F	A	Pts
Spain	8	6	1	1	20	3	13
Rep. Ireland	8	5	2	1	10	2	12
Hungary	8	2	4	2	8	12	8
N. Ireland	8	2	1	5	6	12	5
Malta	8	0	2	6	3	18	2

SPAIN, REP. IRELAND qualify for the finals.

Group 7

	P	W	D	L	F	A	Pts
Belgium	8	4	4	0	15	5	12
Czechoslovakia	8	5	2	1	13	3	12
Portugal	8	4	2	2	11	8	10
Switzerland	8	2	1	5	10	14	5
Luxembourg	8	0	1	7	3	22	1

BELGIUM, CZECHOSLOVAKIA qualify for the finals.

Africa

Group A

	P	W	D	L	F	A	Pts
Algeria	4	3	1	0	6	1	7
Ivory Coast	4	1	2	1	5	1	4
Zimbabwe	4	0	1	3	1	10	1

Group B

	P	W	D	L	F	A	Pts
Egypt	6	3	2	1	6	2	8
Liberia	6	2	2	2	2	3	6
Malawi	6	1	3	2	3	4	5
Kenya	6	1	3	2	2	4	5

Group C

	P	W	D	L	F	A	Pts
Cameroon	6	4	1	1	9	6	9
Nigeria	6	3	1	2	7	5	7
Angola	6	1	2	3	6	7	4
Gabon	6	2	0	4	5	9	4

Group D

	P	W	D	L	F	A	Pts
Tunisia	6	3	1	2	5	5	7
Zambia	6	3	0	3	7	6	6
Zaire	6	2	2	2	7	7	6
Morocco	6	1	3	2	4	5	5

Final qualifying matches

8.10.89	Algeria v Egypt	0–0
8.10.89	Cameroon v Tunisia	2–0
22.10.89	Egypt v Algeria	1–0
19.11.89	Tunisia v Cameroon	0–1

EGYPT (1–0 agg) and
CAMEROON (3–0 agg) qualify for the finals.

Asia

Group 1

	P	W	D	L	F	A	Pts
Qatar	6	3	3	0	8	3	9
Iraq	6	3	2	1	11	5	8
Jordan	6	2	1	3	5	7	5
Oman	6	0	2	4	2	11	2

Group 2

	P	W	D	L	F	A	Pts
S. Arabia	4	3	1	0	7	4	7
Syria	4	2	1	1	7	5	5
Yemen AR	4	0	0	4	0	5	0

Group 3

	P	W	D	L	F	A	Pts
UAE	4	3	0	1	12	4	6
Kuwait	4	3	0	1	6	3	6
Pakistan	4	0	0	4	1	12	0

Group 4

	P	W	D	L	F	A	Pts
South Korea	6	6	0	0	25	0	12
Malaysia	6	3	1	2	8	8	7
Singapore	6	2	1	3	12	9	5
Nepal	6	0	0	6	0	28	0

Group 5

	P	W	D	L	F	A	Pts
China	6	5	0	1	13	3	10
Iran	6	5	0	1	12	5	10
Bangladesh	6	1	0	5	4	9	2
Thailand	6	1	0	5	2	14	2

Group 6

	P	W	D	L	F	A	Pts
North Korea	5	3	1	1	9	4	7
Japan	6	2	3	1	7	3	7
Hong Kong	6	0	3	3	5	10	3
Indonesia	5	1	3	1	4	8	3

Round 2

	P	W	D	L	F	A	Pts
South Korea	5	3	2	0	5	1	8
UAE	5	1	4	0	4	3	6
Qatar	5	1	3	1	4	5	5
China	5	2	0	3	5	6	4
S. Arabia	5	1	2	2	4	5	4
N. Korea	5	1	1	3	2	4	3

SOUTH KOREA, UAE qualify for the finals.

North/Central America

	P	W	D	L	F	A	Pts
Costa Rica	8	5	1	2	10	6	11
United States	8	4	3	1	6	3	10
Trinidad/Tobago	8	3	3	2	7	5	9
Guatemala	6	1	1	4	4	7	3
El Salvador	6	0	2	4	2	8	2

COSTA RICA, UNITED STATES qualify for the finals.

Oceania

	P	W	D	L	F	A	Pts
Israel	4	1	3	0	5	4	5
Australia	4	1	2	1	6	5	4
N. Zealand	4	1	1	2	5	7	3

ISRAEL qualified to play Columbia for place in the finals.

South America

Group 1

	P	W	D	L	F	A	Pts
Uruguay	4	3	0	1	7	2	6
Bolivia	4	3	0	1	6	5	6
Peru	4	0	0	4	2	8	0

URUGUAY qualify for the finals.

Group 2

	P	W	D	L	F	A	Pts
Columbia	4	2	1	1	4	3	5
Paraguay	4	2	0	2	5	6	4
Ecuador	4	1	1	2	3	3	3

COLUMBIA qualified to play Israel for place in the finals.

Group 3

	P	W	D	L	F	A	Pts
Brazil	4	3	1	0	12	2	7
Chile	4	2	1	1	9	4	5
Venezuela	4	0	0	4	2	17	0

BRAZIL qualify for the finals.

South America/Oceania

15.10.89	Columbia v Israel	1–0
30.10.89	Israel v Columbia	0–0

COLUMBIA qualify for the finals.

VIEWS FROM THE STARS

ANDY GORAM – *Hibernian*

Goalkeeping understudy to Jim Leighton, Goram got his big chance against Yugoslavia in the World Cup's last season when he helped Scotland to a 1–1 draw. He began his career at West Bromwich, then moved to Oldham in 1981, and joined Hibernian for £300,000 in 1987.

I think that Italy will do well in this year's World Cup Finals. They have a very talented team with home advantage. Germany, Brazil, Russia and Yugoslavia will also be strong teams and hard to beat.

I think that the footballers who are likely to make the biggest impression in Italy are Gullit, Vialli, Rinat Dassaer, Mo Johnston, Careca, Paul McStay, van Basten, Barnes; these are all proven, world-class players – and, of course, there's sure to be a few more as well.

From previous World Cup Finals, the game I remember most is Scotland *v* Holland in Argentina; Scotland won a great game, with Archie Gemmill scoring one of the best goals of the tournament. Asked whether he thought Scotland would score the three goals they needed against Holland to qualify for the next round, Jongbloed, the Dutch goalkeeper, replied: 'Yes, but not in ninety minutes!'

The Scots played splendidly that day, driven on by Souness and little Archie Gemmill; 1–0 down at one stage, they kept battling away. Dalglish equalised, and Gemmill scored a penalty to make it 2–1. But the goal with which he made it 3–1 was astonishing – Gemmill took the ball from outside his penalty area, swerved around three bemused defenders, and ended with a slashing shot past Jongbloed. Unfortunately, Rep gave Holland a second, vital goal to take them into the next qualifying stage.

My favourite World Cup footballer was Pelé, for obvious reasons. Although I was too young to appreciate his talents, when I watch the old games on film it makes me realise how great he was.

It was important for Scotland to qualify for the Finals. Now it's all down to a bit of luck on the day because, after all, it is a knock-out competition and anything can happen.

I've had a taste of international football; I was on the bench as reserve to Jim Leighton in the Mexico Finals, and it was a great experience. Of all the games I've played in, I'll never forget my debut against East Germany at Hampden because the score was 0–0. Also, it was pleasing to play my first World Cup against Yugoslavia last year, when we drew 1–1.

BRIAN McCLAIR – *Manchester United*

A Manchester United striker, McClair finished last season top scorer at United for the second season in succession since his £850,000 transfer from Celtic in 1987. He is a Scottish international who began his career at Aston Villa before moving to Motherwell and then Celtic.

Italy must have a good chance in the competition because they have a good team, have played together for three years, and have home advantage. You can never write off Brazil because of their great skill, and they also have a good team as they proved in the South American Championship. Holland will also be there, or thereabouts, because they have an exciting football team.

Footballers likely to make a big impact are Gullit, because of his all-round ability, and Stojkovic from Yugoslavia, who is a great passer of the ball, reads a game well and dominates matches. The game from previous World Cup Finals that I remember as being most exciting was when France met West Germany in Spain in 1982.

My personal hopes for next year's competition are that we see some good football, lots of goals and, hopefully, harmony among the supporters.

ANDY ROXBURGH – *Manager, Scotland*

I think Italy will do well this year, because they are an excellent, young team and have the advantage of being the hosts. Argentina can build on their 1986 success in Mexico; Holland have the best squad of players in Europe; and Yugoslavia, with their top-class individual talents, could be a surprise package.

The footballers likely to make the biggest impact are Gullit and van Basten of Holland, Vialli and Baresi of Italy, Maradona of Argentina, Stojkovic and Saviceivic of Yugoslavia. There have been some marvellous games in previous World Cup Finals, especially when France played Brazil in Guadalajara. It was renowned for its brilliant football and wonderful drama – it was only a pity that it had to be decided by kicks from the penalty spot.

My favourite all-time World Cup footballer was Pelé, who won three World Cup winner's medals, scored brilliant goals, was a great artist and, above all, a sportsman. I hope that now that Scotland are one of the finalists, we produce a team which represents the country with credit.

My previous experience of World Cups was when I attended the Finals in Argentina in 1978, as an observer; Archie Gemmill's goal against Holland in Mendoza was the highlight for me. I assisted Jock Stein in Spain in 1982, and the Scotland against Brazil game was magnificent because the atmosphere was like a real carnival. In 1986 I worked as a FIFA technician and it was a great experience meeting all the top players and managers, attending training sessions and being closely involved in the organisation of the matches, up to and including the Final itself. I stood a few feet away from Maradona when he received the Cup in the Aztec Stadium, and wondered if a Scot would ever get close to the trophy some time in the future.

IAN BRANFOOT – *Ex-Manager, Reading*

My predictions for World Cup success are Italy, Brazil and West Germany, with the Italian and Brazilian players likely to make the biggest impact.

The most exciting match I remember from previous competitions was the 1966 Final; the Europeans dominated in their own continent, providing all four semi-finalists. Despite Wolfgang Weber's dramatic late equaliser, Hurst's hat-trick ensured an England victory which I will always remember.

I hope that England are successful in this year's competition and that there are no crowd problems.

ALEX FERGUSON – *Manager, Manchester United*

I think that Italy, Holland and West Germany will do well this summer, with Gullit, van Basten and Baresi likely to make a big impression for Holland and Italy respectively.

I have happy memories of previous World Cup Finals, especially the game between West Germany and Italy in 1970, which Italy won 4–3 after extra time. Italy took the lead after nine minutes through Boninsegna, who had come to Mexico only as a replacement for Anastasi, the most expensive player in the world. Despite an injury to Beckenbauer, the Germans pressed continuously and Schnellinger scored in injury time. Extra time produced five goals, with Rivera deciding the game.

I hope that in Italy there will be no trouble, and that the British teams experience success.

TED CROKER – *Ex-Secretary of the Football Association*

There are several teams who I think will do well in this year's World Cup, including Italy, Portugal, West Germany, Argentina, England and Holland. Johann Cruyff is my favourite World Cup footballer of all time because he was such a talented and inspirational player.

I have been involved in previous World Cups, and I specially remember the England performance in the first phase of the World Cup in Spain in 1982, when we played extremely well. I believe we had our best chance since 1966 of winning the World Cup, but unfortunately both Kevin Keegan and Trevor Brooking, two of our world-class players, were injured and Bryan Robson was nursing a strained groin. We failed to reach the semi-final and the chance had gone. I was bitterly disappointed.

ALAN SMITH – *Arsenal*

Striker Alan was top scorer at Highbury last season, with an impressive 26 goals. He made his full England debut against Greece, and was George Graham's costly signing at £800,000 from Leicester in 1987.

I believe that Italy will do well, partly because they are the home nation and this will be a great advantage, and also because they always have a very well-organised team in the Finals. Also, West Germany always appear to come good for the Finals. Most of all, I think England will make a very good impression.

Undoubtedly, Maradona will have a good time in Italy, and Gullit and van Basten are likely to repeat their European Championship form. From Italy, Vialli looks a great striker.

The game between France and Brazil from the 1986 Finals was the most exciting game I've ever seen. It was a quarter-final match which France won 4–3 on penalties, and involved great individual skills from players like Platini, and some great goals. My favourite World Cup footballer would have to be Pelé, simply because he was such a brilliant all-round player and he played in so many World Cup competitions.

My most memorable moment from previous internationals must be my debut for England when we played Saudi Arabia in the most luxurious stadium I have ever seen. I came on as a substitute, but the following game against Greece was more important to me because I started the game.

I hope that I will be part of Mr Robson's plans when we go to Italy; it would be lovely to get a chance to play in the Finals.

JOHN GREGORY – *Ex-Manager, Portsmouth*

My tips for 1990 are Italy and West Germany, with Vialli and Gullit likely to make the biggest impact. The game I remember most from previous World Cup Finals was when Brazil beat Italy 3–2 in 1982.

My favourite World Cup footballer of all time was Michel Platini of France. Quite simply, my personal hope for next year's competition is that England will win it.

JOHN MOTSON – *BBC Television Commentator*

If I had to make a prediction for the teams to contest the Final, it would be Italy, because they are the host nation, and Holland, because they have Gullit, van Basten and Rijkaard. I am looking forward to commentating on matches which include players of the qualities of Vialli from Italy, Bebeto from Brazil, Litouchnen Einco of the Soviet Union and Vanenburg of Holland.

As a commentator, the most exciting game for me was Italy 3 Brazil 2 in Barcelona in 1982; Italy had to win to reach the semi-final and knock out Brazil, and had to take the lead three times in order to do so.

My favourite players in the sixties and seventies were Franz Beckenbauer, now manager, and Michel Platini. My favourite manager was Guy Thys from Belgium, who was a great survivor.

I'm looking forward immensely to commentating for the BBC for this year's competition, and I only hope that there are no crowd disturbances and that there is plenty of fast, attractive and attacking football to comment upon, and above all, plenty of good sportsmanship. This will be my fifth World Cup as a commentator, having represented the BBC in West Germany, Argentina, Spain and Mexico.

STEVE HARRISON – *Manager, Watford*

Several teams could do very well this summer, but I go for Italy because they are good defensively, West Germany for their all-round strength, England because they are solid and also after their failure in the European Championships have something to prove, and Holland because they have very confident players.

I'm looking forward to seeing players from the Middle Eastern countries, and they may surprise people by making a good impression.

Like most Englishmen I remember the 1966 World Cup Final as being something special, but 1970 was even better because of Brazil's breathtaking performance. I think that Pelé was the best player in the world for twenty years, and my favourite manager was Sir Alf Ramsey because he combined originality with ability.

The scene is set for a great competition with some open and attractive football, and we keep our fingers crossed that there will be no trouble on or off the field.

ARTHUR COX – *Manager, Derby County*

My only prediction for this year's World Cup champions is England, with Beardsley and Robson both likely to make a big impression. Holland have some good players, including Rijkaard and Koeman, and Argentina, of course, have Maradona.

I'm looking forward immensely to the Finals of the competition, because I think the final stages stand out in everyone's mind as the most thrilling in all World Cups.

Of all the managers I have met, Helmut Schoen from West Germany has my vote as the all-time great. Unfortunately, I've never had the privilege of being involved in world competitions, but I sincerely hope that that is something which I achieve in the future.

DAVID NISH – *Coach, Middlesbrough FC*

Italy, with home advantage, must be strong contenders for world champions this year; Brazil, having triumphed in the South American Cup, won't be far behind, and of course, West Germany can never be ruled out.

Players to watch for are Maradona, with his obvious outstanding skills, van Basten, a superb goal-scorer, Gullit, always likely to be a match winner, and Careca, another exciting goal-scorer.

The best Final that I've ever seen was in 1970, with Brazil being the team with outstanding skill and flair – their free kicks in particular. It was a tremendous victory over Italy in the Final.

I had the privilege of playing against Franz Beckenbauer late on in his career, and it was only then that I realised what 'world class' meant.

I hope that this year's competition is trouble-free, and that the best footballing and most skilful team wins the competition.

EDDY NIEDZWIECKI – *Coach, Chelsea*

Italy will probably do well this year and fulfil the potential of a team which has played as a unit for two years; West Germany have the discipline, and Argentina the skill and organisation. I'm looking forward to watching Vialli from Italy, who is an exciting and individual player.

My favourite World Cup footballer was Johann Cruyff, who had unbelievable talent, and I also admire Holland's Rinus Michels for the way that his side plays. I hope that football comes out as the winner in Italy, and not violence.

As a player I was on the bench on both occasions when Wales played Scotland at home and away in 1984. I experienced the elation of winning in Scotland 1–0, and also the disappointment of not qualifying as a result of a draw in the return match. The penalty seven minutes from time robbed us.

FRED STREET – *England Physiotherapist*

Traditionally the winners are from the home zone, i.e. a European side wins in Europe, South Americans in South America, but this year I fancy that Argentina may upset the sequence. I hope that Bryan Robson and company make the biggest impression in Italy, though.

A game that I was involved with in previous Finals was our match against Spain in 1982; we scored after only 27 seconds in Bilbao, with Bryan Robson scoring the first two England goals. Had he not injured a groin in the next match, then I believe that England would have done even better in that year's competition.

It would be marvellous to see England win in Italy, as long as they play attractive football in the process; but win or lose, let us all hope for sporting and orderly supporters.

I have been England's physiotherapist and trainer for four World Cup competitions, and now that they have qualified for Italy this will be my third World Cup Finals, plus two European Nations' Cup Finals. I'm really looking forward to it.

FRANK CLARK – *Manager, Leyton Orient*

It is almost impossible to predict the outcome of this World Cup competition, because so many countries have the players capable of winning the competition. I only hope that all matches pass off relatively trouble-free as far as crowds are concerned, and that the games themselves are a feast of attacking football.

BOBBY ROBSON – *Manager, England*

As a midfield provider, Bobby spurred England's forwards to remarkable feats in 1960–61, and later in the 1960s as a manager he took Ipswich back into Division

One. His twenty internationals, which included the 1958 World Cup, came during a six-year stay at West Bromwich that was sandwiched between spells at Fulham. As England manager, his opinions about Italy are very significant.

The countries I think will do well are Italy, USSR, Argentina, Brazil and 'dark horses' Belgium. It goes without saying that England hope to do well also!

Every World Cup produces players who were previously unknown but who come into prominence during the tournament, and this is arguably so with many countries, Brazil being a good example. However, I still feel that the really great players will shine, i.e. Maradona, Gullit, van Basten, Rijkaard and Vialli.

The matches from previous World Cup Finals I remember as the most exciting are England's World Cup win against West Germany in 1966, France against West Germany and Spain in 1982, and Belgium versus USSR and Mexico in 1986.

As an international manager the players I would most like to have had in my team are Pelé and Garrincha.

My personal hope for this year's competition is that we go as far as we can and that our players play to their utmost ability. We got to the final eight on the last occasion, and we want to improve on that.

I enjoyed being involved in international matches as a player, and I remember that when we played Scotland at Wembley in 1961, and won 9–3, I scored the first goal. I played again at Wembley against Spain in 1960, a match that we won 4–2.

Out of my World Cup experiences, England against Brazil in Sweden in 1958 stands out; we drew 0–0 in a very technical game during which players cancelled each other out. It was the only point Brazil dropped and the only time that they failed to score.

JIM SMITH – *Manager, Newcastle United*

My predictions for World Cup success are Italy, Brazil, West Germany, Holland and Russia. Watch out for players with the quality of Gullit, Alofs, Maradona and Vialli.

I hope that England win, and that there are no crowd problems.

BILLY McNEIL – *Manager, Celtic*

If I were a gambling man I would bet on Brazil, Italy, Yugoslavia and West Germany to do well in this year's competition. I'm looking forward to seeing the players with the quality of Vialli, Donadoni and Maldini from Italy, McStay from Scotland, and Stojkovic and Katenec from Yugoslavia.

I still remember the 1970 Final, when Brazil beat Italy 4–1 because Carlos Alberto exploited his right flank with overlapping runs, while Gerson and Clodaldo controlled midfield – they won by playing adventurous football.

Obviously, I hope that Scotland will progress beyond the first round. The highlight of my own international career was when Scotland beat England in 1962 at Hampden. This stands out in my mind because it was the first Scottish win over England in Scotland for twenty-five years.

KENNY DALGLISH – *Player-Manager, Liverpool*

Quite simply, Italy will win the World Cup and Vialli will make his presence felt.

In 1982 the West Germany *v* France game is one that I will always remember with great fondness.

My favourite World Cup footballer of all time is Pelé, and with regard to this year's competition, my personal hope is that we have plenty of entertainment.

GRAEME SOUNESS – *Manager, Glasgow Rangers*

Italy is my tip for World Cup champions.

The game I remember most from previous World Cup Finals was the game when France played West Germany in the semi-final match in Spain in 1986. Pelé was my favourite World Cup footballer and I remember when he played in Mexico in 1970 in one very remarkable forward-line.

My personal hope for this year's competition is to see some of the greatest players playing in a country where football is fully appreciated.

The highlight of my own career was being captain for Scotland against Brazil in Spain.

TONY MOWBRAY – *Middlesbrough*

I think Brazil will do well, because I've seen them on 'Eurosport' and they look very impressive. Italy are my second choice, and I think that Romario will score a hatful of goals. As a youngster I remember when England played Brazil in 1970; the game proved to be a fascinating battle, rich in the skills of football. Brazil had lost only once to England in seven previous meetings. Early on, Pelé from Jairzinho's centre headed down to produce an excellent piece of reflex goalkeeping – one of the best ever World Cup saves. Jairzinho scored in the second half and Brazil held on to the lead, despite the ball hitting the woodwork twice and Astle squandering a chance. In 1978 Mario Kempes of Argentina was sheer magic to watch – very exciting every time he got the ball.

I hope that England have a good tournament and that we see some exciting football, with flair overcoming cynicism. I have been involved in the game at international level during the England B tour of Switzerland, Iceland and Norway in May 1989, and it was a great thrill just to wear an England shirt.

KEITH HOUCHEN – *Hibernian*

Keith began his career at Chesterfield, but was given a free transfer in 1978. The Hibs striker then played for Hartlepool, Orient, York and Scunthorpe before joining Coventry for £60,000 in 1986.

My predictions for 1990 are Italy, as host country, England, West Germany and Argentina, as holders. I'm looking forward to seeing skilful, exciting players such as Gascoigne, Donadoni of Italy, and Maradona from Argentina.

I remember being enthralled during the game between Russia and Belgium which Belgium won by the odd goal in seven in the 1986 tournament, which was famous for its great goals.

My favourite manager of all time was Alf Ramsey, because he won the World Cup for England and built his reputation on the fact of being a players' man and well respected. Let's hope we have goals, excitement and fun this year.

TREVOR SENIOR – *Reading*

Holland will do well in the tournament because they have good, all-round team performance plus the added bonus of van Basten and Gullit; I also fancy Italy, because they are the home country.

I'm looking forward to watching Maradona, captain of club and country, because he is such a classy, individual player, who led Napoli to their first ever championship victory.

I hope that some of the games in this year's competition live up to the 1982 France against West Germany semi-final for its great entertainment and world-class football. If this year's competition is good entertainment, it will encourage a lot more youngsters to take up the game.

BRYAN ROBSON – *Manchester United and England captain*

Bryan is the influential captain of Manchested United and England who cost £1.5 million from West Bromwich in 1981, a vast amount of money at that time. Bryan made his League debut for West Brom at York in 1975. Currently a midfield player, it is likely that he will move into the heart of Manchester United's defence before the end of the season.

I think that Holland and Argentina will be in the forefront in Italy, with Maradona and Gullit making the biggest impact. As a kid I was greatly influenced by the World Cup Final of 1966, when England played West Germany in a dramatic affair. Germany marked man-for-man with Beckenbauer shadowing Charlton, a move that wasted the German's midfield talent. Alan Ball was tireless in that match in midfield, Moore was immaculate at the back, while Banks made fine saves from Overath and Emmerich. It was unfortunate that the match was decided by what will always be, despite all available evidence, a hotly disputed goal, but it was a remarkable and important victory for England.

I hope that England win this year's World Cup competition. I only hope that I can do as well as I did in 1982 when I scored two goals against France in a game which we won 3–1.

STEVE HODGE – *Nottingham Forest*

England international Steve returned to the City ground for his second spell at the club at the start of last season, at a cost of £550,000. He signed his professional forms with Nottingham Forest in 1980, moving to Aston Villa for £450,000 in 1985 and then to Tottenham Hotspur.

Steve's predictions are Holland, West Germany, Argentina and Italy as the countries most likely to do well in this year's Cup Finals. He vividly remembers the France *v* West Germany semi-final in 1982, won by West Germany on penalties. The Germans had come from two goals behind to level the score during extra time.

His favourite players are Diego Maradona, Pelé and Cruyff. His personal hopes for this year's competition are to be involved, and for England to gain at least a top-four position. Steve has already played for England against Poland, Paraguay and Argentina during 1988, and vividly remembers the playing of the national anthem before the World Cup quarter-final against Argentina, which he says ' . . . was a very proud moment for me'.

JIM BEGLIN – *Leeds United*

Italy will do well because they're on home soil; West Germany are always a force; Holland has the best footballing side in Europe; and Argentina will be very hard to beat.

The footballers I look forward to watching most are Maradona, because if he's on form he is impossible to mark; Gullit, who has sheer class with awesome energy, power and strength; van Basten is a great goal-scorer with class players around him who create lots of chances.

I hope this year's Final is as good as the one in 1970 when Brazil beat Italy with a great side full of big stars including Pelé, Rivelino and Jairzinho. The scenes which followed were unbelievable, with the Brazilians being mobbed as if they had won in Rio. They had played soccer with artistry, skill, virtuosity and grace – real exhibition stuff.

As a defender myself, I'll have to nominate Beckenbauer as my favourite World Cup footballer because he never panicked, always staying cool, had more time on the ball, and made great runs from defence to attack.

I hope that this season I have played well enough with Leeds to win a place in the Republic of Ireland squad, in order to use the Finals to fully resurrect my international career. I've only played in World Cup qualifiers, my most memorable moment being Man of the Match Award as best player on my World Cup debut against Denmark in Copenhagen in November 1984.

STEVE GRITT – *Walsall*

Bournemouth-born Steve played in every position for Charlton Athletic, including goalkeeper, before moving to Walsall. An accomplished cricketer, Steve has represented Hampshire Second XI. His opinions are always worthy of consideration.

Italy will be hard to beat this year, because they know their own grounds; West Germany are always difficult opposition wherever they play; Holland will be keen to maintain their European Championship standard of 1988; and Brazil always seem to produce good footballing teams for World Cups.

Footballers to watch out for are Marco van Basten, who showed true potential in the European Championships, and Bryan Robson, who will want to impress in what will probably be his last World Cup.

As an Englishman it was a proud moment watching England's victory over West Germany in 1966, the only time that England had ever won the competition. I also remember the 1974 Final between Holland and West Germany, when Holland probably played the best football during the tournament but Germany's true professionalism won it in the end – two superb teams. I think that the Brazilian team that won the Cup in 1970 must go down as one of the greatest ever, and I always enjoy watching the way they play throughout the tournament.

I hope that the football played by all the teams is what makes the headlines in the media, and not the stupidity of some so-called supporters. I also hope that England can have a good World Cup to help erase memories of the 1988 European Championships.

STUART PEARCE – *Nottingham Forest*

The England left-back was ever present for his country last season. He joined Nottingham Forest from Coventry for £250,000, having begun his career at Wealdstone. He made his League debut for Coventry against Queen's Park Rangers in 1983. Stuart is currently Nottingham Forest's club captain.

Italy must be firm favourites as host nation and a good team with plenty of home support. West Germany and Holland are much improved nations and the European climate will suit them; Brazil, of course, always do well in World Cup competitions. Gullit and Maradona are both used to playing in Italy and are the best players in the world at the moment.

I've seen some tremendous World Cup matches, but the Belgium against Russia game in 1986 tops the lot, when Belgium won 4–3. It was one of the best games of the competition in terms of skill, excitement and commitment. It was end-to-end play, with Russia taking the lead through Belanov in the twenty-seventh minute. Inspired by Ceulemans, Belgium fought hard to equalise through Scifo. Both sides scored again and it was 2–2 at full time. In extra time, Belgium took a 4–2 lead before Russia pulled a goal back through Belanov, who became the first Russian to score a World Cup hat-trick.

My favourite World Cup footballers are Maradona and Pelé, because to show that you're a cut above the rest, at that level, is something special. Alf Ramsey is my favourite manager, because winning the World Cup says it all.

If I'm in Italy this summer playing for England, then that will make my day. My limited experience at international level is best remembered for my first cap against Brazil at Wembley, and also for beating Scotland at Hampden 2–0.

PAUL POWER – *Everton*

I think Holland will do well because they have quality in every department of the team, particularly Koeman, Rijkaard, Gullit and van Basten. If they all play well together, they will score goals and be difficult to beat – Gullit in particular, because his pace, power and ability in the air mean he can create things for his own team and also stop other teams playing. I am old enough to remember the Brazil *v* Hungary match of 1966 as a classic, because it was an open, exciting game with excellent goals and the result was totally unexpected – Hungary 3 Brazil 1 in group 3. Brazil, with Gerson fit but with Tostao replacing the injured Pelé, suffered their first World Cup defeat since 1954, when their conquerers had been the very same country. Bene scored after three minutes, Tostao levelled and then, in the second half, Albert rampant exposed the Brazilians. Farcas hit a perfect volley and then Meszoly made it 3–1 with a penalty, after a fine run by Bene had been illegally stopped.

Even today my favourite player is Johann Cruyff, because he invented his famous turn which everybody copies now; an exciting player who worked tremendously hard for the Dutch team.

For this year's competition I'm looking forward to seeing great individual skills and great goals. It will be a bonus if it is trouble-free from English supporters, so that English clubs may soon be back in Europe.

MALCOLM MACDONALD – *Ex-Manager, Fulham and Huddersfield*

In his first season at Fulham, Malcolm, who played at full-back, experienced the despair of relegation. In July 1969 he moved to Luton for £17,500, and quickly developed into a natural and prolific goal-scorer. Luton won promotion from the Third Division, with Mac scoring sensational goals along the way. After he had made 30 Second Division goals, Newcastle United manager, the late Joe Harvey, paid £180,000 for his services. In his League debut at St James's against Liverpool, Mac scored a tremendous hat-trick which guaranteed him hero status with the fans. By 1973 he was a full England international, and he went on to win 14 caps.

The four teams I think will do best this summer are Belgium, West Germany, Italy and Brazil. Watch out for Marco van Basten from AC Milan and Holland.

From previous competitions my favourite player was Albert from Hungary. In the 1962 competition he scored a brilliant hat-trick as the Hungarians trounced Belgium 6–1 in a group 4 match.

My favourite manager, whom I played for, was Sir Alf Ramsey. We never feared anyone under Alf; he always made us think that we were the best team in the world: 'You are England players, and we are the best,' he would say. 'The rest of the world respect us, they want to beat us; don't let them.' He commanded respect and always treated the players like men. If Alf punished you it hurt him to do it, but it meant that you always deserved it.

The highlight of my international career was when I scored five goals against Cyprus at Wembley, a game which England won 5–0. If someone had said to me at the start of my career, 'One day you are going to score five goals for England in an international at Wembley,' I would have paid him a fortune to make it come true. At the end of the game, the giant Wembley scoreboard lit up the message: 'SUPER-MAC 5 – CYPRUS 0' – I had written my name into the record books.

I hope that we see an abundance of good football in Italy, and plenty of excitement with no terrace trouble.

LIAM BRADY – *West Ham United*

I think Italy will do well in 1990, as host nation; Holland have class players, and Brazil are the best of the South American sides. Watch out for van Basten, top scorer in Holland with Ajax for four successive seasons before captaining them to the

1987 UEFA Cup – and then moving with Gullit to Milan, for £2 million. Vialli and Baggio from Italy will also be dangerous opponents.

I hope that the competition this year is free from violence on and off the pitch, and that we have a good standard of refereeing. I have never played in the final stages of the World Cup, but hope to make it with the Republic this year.

KEVIN McALLISTER – *Chelsea*

Kevin looked set to leave Stamford Bridge after failing to gain a first-team place, but the departure of Nevin and Wegerle gave him his chance. The flying winger cost £34,000 from Falkirk.

I expect Italy and Holland to make the biggest impact. It is always difficult to predict which players are going to be the most remarkable because there are always several unknowns who take centre stage.

The best game I've seen in World Cup tournaments so far was the semi-final between France and West Germany in 1986. It was a re-run of that in 1982, and though it provided the same result it produced far more excitement. A mistake from the French keeper Bats let in Brehme, with substitute Voller scoring a second goal in the final minute to take West Germany to their second consecutive Final.

Let's hope that we see some good, exciting games in Italy which are trouble-free both on and off the pitch.

PAUL DAVIS – *Arsenal*

Davis made his England debut against Denmark, and looked set for a great season until injury and suspension restricted him to eleven League games. He is a former Highbury apprentice who signed professional forms in 1979.

Brazil, Holland and Italy are my favourite countries for the Cup; the quality of their players is very high. Holland and Italy are progressing very well, and Brazil will always make their mark because of the way they play.

DAVID SEAMAN – *Queen's Park Rangers*

The Queen's Park Rangers goalkeeper already has one cap to his credit in the 1–1 draw against Saudia Arabia in November 1988. He has been on the England bench for several internationals since then. Standing 6 feet 3 inches tall, he was capped ten times for the England Under-21 side. David began his League career with Peterborough before moving to QPR from Birmingham for £225,000 in August 1986.

I think that England will do well in the World Cup Finals because we have a strong squad and are playing confidently at the moment. Also with a good chance are Italy, who have the advantage of playing in their own country and gaining maximum support.

Maradona and Gullit are both key men in their particular sides, because of the tremendous amount of skill which they possess. Bryan Robson is likely to make a big impact because of his strong will to win.

In the 1986 Final between Argentina and West Germany both teams played as well as each other, and the deciding goal for the South Americans was something very special. Maradona is a very exciting player to watch because he has so much skill and strength.

I hope that England have a successful competition and that I get a chance to be involved. Making my debut in Saudi Arabia has been the highlight of my own career so far.

TONY DORIGO – *Chelsea*

This twenty-four-year-old Chelsea player has made eleven Under-21 appearances. When capped at senior level he will become the first native Australian (born in Melbourne) to win full England honours. As a boy of fifteen Tony paid his own air fare to have trials with Aston Villa, who launched him on his career. His transfer from Villa cost Chelsea £745,000 in May 1987.

Italy will be the team to beat because they have groomed younger players into the side over the last three years, in readiness for 1990. They are on home soil, they have experience and know-how from winning the World Cup in 1982, and must have a great chance of winning. Other teams to watch out for are Brazil, West Germany and England.

Vialli of Italy could come into his own on home soil. Careca of Brazil, Gullit and van Basten of Holland, as well as being outstanding talents, have the advantage of currently playing in Italy.

I only hope this year's Final is as exciting as the one in 1982 between Italy and West Germany in Spain, when Rossi emerged the hero.

I hope that I am in the England squad that goes to Italy, because to play in the World Cup would be a dream come true, and to win it would be even better! I have been involved in international matches before, for example the European Championship when England played Holland when I was in the squad but not playing. Just watching Gullit and van Basten's goals was memorable enough.

COLIN GIBSON – *Manchester United*

A defender who began his career at Aston Villa, Colin won a League Championship medal with them in 1981 before joining Manchester United in 1985 for £250,000.

On form, I would probably go for Holland, although West Germany, Italy, Argentina and Brazil are also strong possibilities. Out of these five, I suspect that Brazil might not do as well in comparison with the four other teams who have proven track records.

Obviously Maradona, Gullit, van Basten and Koeman are the footballers who are most likely to make an impact in Italy. Rijkaard of Holland and Vialli of Italy are the two European players who should also play well in the Finals.

Pelé is undoubtedly my favourite World Cup footballer because he stands for everything that the World Cup is about – most of all, the coming together of all footballing nations.

NEVILLE SOUTHALL – *Everton*

Neville's distinguished performances in goal for non-league Winsford United put him on the road to success in full-time professional football, when Bury signed him for £6000 in 1980. After only one season, Neville was signed by Everton for £150,000.

I'm sure that Argentina, West Germany and Italy are the countries who will have the greatest success in the 1990 World Cup. Not England although, even as a Welshman, I remember their 1966 win as the most exciting game from previous World Cup Finals.

Of course, I've never played in the Finals although I have had some memorable moments in international matches. I particularly recall when I played for Wales in an away game against Holland, even though we lost 1–0, and also following a close second was the friendly match held at Cardiff, when Wales drew 1–1 with Brazil.

In next year's football season, and in the World Cup, I would very much hope to see exciting football, good sportsmanship and a higher level of refereeing in general.

NEIL WEBB – *Manchester United*

Neil was an attacking midfield force in Nottingham
Forest's excellent 1988–89 campaign, before transfer-
ring to Manchester United. He began his career with his
home-town club Reading, where his father Doug had
been a forward from 1956 to 1966.

I would expect Italy to do very well in the 1990 World Cup
Finals because they are the host country and offer an excellent
team of up-and-coming young players. Holland usually excel
in big competitions and, of course, I think England should do
well.
   I think that the footballers who are likely to make the
greatest impact in Italy are Ruud Gullit, because he is such a
good all-round player, and Vialli because of his immense skill
in the game.
   The Italy *v* Brazil match which resulted in a 4–3 win for
Italy is without a doubt the most exciting football match ever
played. The level of skill was extremely high and the goals
scored were brilliant.
   In my opinion, Pelé is the greatest footballer of all time and
he has been my hero since I was a young boy. I was privileged
to meet him when I played in the League Centenary Match.

CHRIS HUGHTON – *Tottenham Hotspur*

Born on 11 December 1958 in Forest Gate, Chris joined
Spurs as a youngster and signed professional forms in
1976. A Republic of Ireland international, Chris fulfilled
his potential in the European Championships in 1988.

Mainly, I think that Italy will do well because the team
consists of quality players who will react well under the
pressure of playing at home. Brazil's team always do well, and
West Germany's experience will stand them in good stead. It is
so long since the England team achieved anything that I think
it may be their turn to win.

The footballers likely to make the biggest impact are Careca of Brazil, Vialli of Italy, van Basten, Ruud Gullit and Rijkaard of Holland, and Chris Waddle and Paul Gascoigne of England.

My favourite World Cup footballer is definitely Pelé. He was an outstanding all-round player and I have always admired his style. Tele Santana of Brazil must follow a close second.

Chris has a great many memories from the international matches in which he has played, not least from the Republic's win over England in the 1988 European Championships.

It was the first time we had qualified, and to actually win meant a great deal to the Irish supporters.

MARK McGHEE – *Newcastle United*

My predictions for the four semi-finalists in the 1990 World Cup Finals have to be Yugoslavia, West Germany, Italy and Brazil.

Without needing to name any names, the footballers who are most likely to cause the greatest impact in the Finals will be those who have the best passing ability and good first touch with the ball.

I personally think that the Argentina *v* Holland World Cup Final remains the most exciting game from previous tournaments. And my favourite World Cup footballer of all time? It's got to be Diego Maradona.

I hope that Scotland play well, and that the team play against the Republic of Ireland in the Final! A goal in that match would be nice. Scoring for my team in the Scotland *v* England match is the most memorable moment of my footballing career so far.

MICHAEL A. FLYNN – *Oldham Athletic*

The Italians will have to make an impact – playing on home soil, they probably daren't not do well!

HOWARD WILKINSON – *Manager, Leeds United*

Manager for Sheffield Wednesday, and then for Leeds United, Howard Wilkinson has some very outspoken views on the World Cup Finals.

I'm positive that West Germany and Italy are the two teams likely to achieve greatest success in the forthcoming 1990 World Cup Finals. As for individual players . . . the successful ones will be the good ones, whoever they may be. Mark my words, one or two names will emerge. But I don't expect them to challenge Pelé for the title of the greatest footballer of all time.

The best thing that could happen to football next year would be to have no crowd trouble, and to see great football being played. As a boy I was picked for the England Under-18 and this has to be one of my most memorable moments. To this day my first game at Swindon is still crystal-clear.

FRANK STAPLETON – *Blackburn Rovers*

The countries with the strongest teams and the best players are Holland, Argentina, Italy and Brazil, so I would predict that any one of these teams has a great chance of winning the World Cup Finals in 1990.

I think that the best players include Maradona of Argentina, Careca of Brazil, and van Basten and Gullit from Holland.

Thinking back, an all-action match showing great skill and plenty of goals was the game between France and West Germany in 1982.

My most memorable matches at international level were those in the European Nations' tournament of 1988, in West Germany, when we were so close to reaching the semi-finals.

DOUG ROUGVIE – *Dunfermline Athletic*

The winners? The tournament is wide open – it could even be
Scotland! The Dutch players are very good, and there is always
the chance that new stars will emerge from Spain, Brazil or
Italy.

From previous tournaments I recall, in 1982, when Italy
needed to beat Brazil to reach the semi-finals. In the end they
won 3–2, and Rossi scored a hat-trick.

I would have to say Pelé is my favourite World Cup
footballer because of his involvement in campaigns and the
enjoyment he brings to so many people.

MAURICE MALPAS – *Dundee United*

Italy are playing in their own back garden so I think they
should do well. Russia, assuming they qualify, and Yugoslavia
are also possibilities because they are geared up for big
occasions.

Any footballers who score the goals will achieve glory for
themselves and their teams.

The Brazil *v* England match held in Mexico in 1970 with the
unbelievable save from Gordon Banks off a Pelé header makes
it one of my best-remembered games of all time.

It would be great to see football like that again this year –
free from crowd troubles. Personally, I just want to be part of
the Scotland squad in Italy.

RICHARD GOUGH – *Glasgow Rangers*

One footballer whom I expect to create a big impact in Italy is
Dragon Stojkovic of Yugoslavia.

My favourite World Cup footballer of all time is Franz
Beckenbauer.

As regards next year's competition, my personal hopes are
just to get there.

TREVOR FRANCIS – *Ex-Player-Manager, Queen's Park Rangers*

Inevitably, I think that both Italy and Brazil are in with a good chance.

All I hope for next year is for England to win the competition.

PAUL GODDARD – *Millwall*

I would hope for fair competition, attractive football and for many goals to be scored.

I have many memorable moments, including my one and only full cap. It is just a great honour to play for your country.

COLIN FOSTER – *West Ham United*

It will mainly be the strikers of the top teams who cause the most impact.

One of the best World Cup footballers is Franz Beckenbauer – brilliant in the tackle, good in the air, and what a ball player!

NIGEL SPINK – *Aston Villa*

I think England will do well, mainly because I am very loyal, and also because you have to believe they will win every game!

It is always the goal-scorers who are remembered in these competitions, so perhaps Maradona will be spotlighted again.

BRUCE RIOCH – *Manager, Middlesbrough*

West Germany, Italy and Brazil should do well in the 1990 Finals, possibly Brazil to win the World Cup.

Vialli of Italy and Careca and Bebeto of Brazil will probably be the star players of the World Cup Finals.

The most exciting and enjoyable match I have ever seen was the Brazil game in 1970 against Italy. Before that, I have seen films of the 1958 Brazilian World Cup Team and they were also outstanding.

My favourite football manager is Alf Ramsey, because he lifted football out of the gutter and put it back on the world stage. He fully deserved his knighthood and the honour it entailed.

Most of all, I would like to see an 'attack-minded' World Cup Final. If the tournament could be free of violence, both on and off the field, it would be great. I would also enjoy seeing one of the Third World countries producing shock results.

Obviously, my most memorable moments are beating England at Wembley in 1977 2–1, and captaining the Scotland team.

STEVE NICOL – *Liverpool*

My bets are on Italy and Argentina, mainly because they both have good players who play well together as a team.

The Argentina *v* Peru match which resulted in a 6–0 win for Argentina is the match which I remember as being the most exciting.

Ally McLeod is still my favourite football manager of all time.

STEVE COPPELL – *Manager, Crystal Palace*

For obvious reasons, my all-time favourite football match was the England *v* West Germany World Cup Final of 1966.

Like most other people in England, my personal hopes for next year are to see a trouble-free World Cup tournament.

DAVE SEXTON – *Manager, England Youth Team*

I remember two particular matches from previous World Cup Finals as being incredibly exciting; the France *v* West Germany semi-final of 1982 held in Spain, and the Italy *v* West Germany semi-final of 1970 held in Mexico.

My personal hopes for the forthcoming World Cup in 1990 are to see England reach the Final – and win it!

STEVE CLARKE – *Chelsea*

Perhaps Yugoslavia will be the dark horses of the tournament. Having seen them in the qualifying games, they appear to be a very well-organised and talented team.

My personal hopes are simply that football is the winner. I hope that once the tournament is over, the talk is of great games and players, not about the problems which are currently ruining the sport.

There are many obvious superstars, but after the World Cup I suspect that Dragon Stojkovic of Yugoslavia may well be the name on everybody's tongue.

TONY GALVIN – *Swindon Town*

The footballers whom I would expect to make an impact in Italy include Klinsman of West Germany, Rijkaard of Holland, Zavarov of the Soviet Union, Stojkovic of Yugoslavia and, of course, John Barnes.

Now that Eire have qualified my first ambition is to be part of the squad. I'm sure that once we reach the Finals, we will be able to give a good account of ourselves.

163

BOB WILSON – *BBC Television Commentary Team*

It will take a very special team to beat the host nation, Italy, although Brazil or Argentina could perhaps do it. England should do much better than they have done recently, and I would expect them to reach the semi-finals at least.

Maradona, who equals Pelé and Cruyff when playing to his full potential, should cause an impact. The Italian Vialli should be mature enough to sustain consistency and any one of several young Brazilians could also create a stir.

I would select Sir Alf Ramsey as my all-time favourite manager for his blunt and outspoken confidence.

Mainly, I would like to see the quality of the 1970 Finals in Mexico repeated; they were the most entertaining of previous World Cup matches I have seen.

STEVE HARDWICK – *Huddersfield Town*

A former England Youth international, Steve began his professional career with Chesterfield before moving to Newcastle United in 1977. He joined Oxford United in 1983 and made 129 consecutive appearances, helping them to win the Third Division title and, later, promotion to the First Division.

Steve joined Huddersfield Town two seasons ago, linking up with former team-mate Peter Withe, the assistant manager.

I feel that the usual major countries will be at the forefront, that's Italy, Brazil, Argentina and England. The Italians have some very exciting young players including Roberto Baggio and Roberto Donadoni.

My hope is that the tournament is open and attacking and the rewards go to the most adventurous teams.

ONE PLAYER'S WORLD CUP

David McCreery, Hearts and Northern Ireland

Q *In which World Cup Finals did you participate?*

A Spain, in 1982, and Mexico four years later. Unfortunately, Northern Ireland did not qualify this time around, so I'm not going to be playing in Italy.

Q *In your opinion, who were the outstanding players in the Finals in which you did play?*

A Well, the French players made a great impression in Spain, and I especially remember Platini and Giresse. Everyone was raving about Platini's skill and expected him to play well. I still think that Maradona was the most impressive player in Mexico, along with Junor and Careca of Brazil – I'm definitely going to watch out for Careca in Italy because he is playing so well at the moment.

AMAZING FACT

The highest number of goals scored by one player in one Finals series is 13 by Just Fontaine (France) in the 1958 tournament. He scored in each match. Two other players have scored in every game in the Finals: Jairzinho (Brazil) in 1970, and Alcide Ghiggia (Uruguay) in 1950. Jairzinho scored 7 goals, Ghiggia 4.

Q *What do you think makes a good international player?*

A There is a huge difference between playing a game on a Saturday afternoon and playing for your country, so I believe that significant adjustments need to be made. International soccer is played at a much more measured pace in comparison with the English or Scottish Leagues. Because you join an elite group when playing for your country, the level of skill is extremely high, and it is essential to fit in with a new style of play: a build-up of play from the back which breaks quickly on the counter-attack.

Q *What are the qualities to look for in a good international manager?*

A A manager who can get the best out of his players will always do well. The squad usually meets on the Sunday prior to an international match, and stays together for a few days. Above all, a manager must know and understand his players and be capable of relaxing them, whilst at the same time gearing them up to play in a match.

Q *Whom do you believe to be the international managers of the future?*

A It's a very difficult area to predict because managers of the home countries tend to stay around for a long time. Steve Coppell would be my bet for a future England boss because he is respected within the game and has a good track record at Crystal Palace.

Q *What do you think of refereeing in general?*

A I'm positive that mistakes can be, and are, made by referees, proved by the infamous 'hand ball' incident with Maradona, which knocked England out of the last Finals. Overall, though, we have the best referees in the world, and standards reflect that.

During the 1954 World Cup Finals Scotland lost both
their games, the first to Austria 1–0 and the second 7–0
to Uruguay. Prior to that match the Scotland manager,
Andy Beattie, had announced that he intended to resign.
He could not really be blamed for Scotland's performance, for he was only one member of the selection
committee and, in any case, only thirteen players had
been taken to Switzerland!

Q *How is it possible for a manager to sustain his team's
morale when players are too often cooped up for
long periods of time during the Finals?*

A With some difficulty, I can assure you! I distinctly
remember the Northern Ireland team being together
for six weeks before the first match had kicked off in
Mexico. During the first three weeks, which served
as the acclimatisation period, our manager arranged
for videos, games and quizzes to help pass the time.
Apart from that, there was little else to do other than
eat and sleep. Luckily, once the competition starts,
the boredom is immediately relieved by watching the
games.

Q *Could you describe for us a typical day in the World
Cup Finals?*

A Obviously, we'd try to make the best use of the
facilities in the first-class hotels we stayed in,
especially the swimming pool. Sunbathing was
allowed, but players were expected to be sensible
and not over-expose themselves, and of course
alcohol was strictly forbidden, except for the odd
half of lager after a game. The mornings would be
set aside for running and stamina work, also helping
us to adjust to the heat, whilst soccer matches and
tactical play took up most of the afternoons.

Q *To what extent do you think football players see the World Cup as a chance to make money?*

A I honestly believe that money is of secondary importance when compared with the honour and satisfaction in having played for your country. There is a 'players' pool' and sponsorship deals are shared amongst the team, as well as payments from the Football Association for qualifying for the Finals.

Q *Whom would you rate as the best Northern Ireland World Cup campaigner?*

A Gerry Armstrong, for scoring vital goals in Spain, and of course big Pat Jennings, who played for his country when he was over forty years of age. It's a great shame that George Best never had a world stage on which to perform and show his marvellous talent.

Q *Do you believe that the success of the 1966 England team, under Sir Alf Ramsey, influenced the overall development of world soccer?*

A Yes, tactically, it was a very significant victory. Alan Ball broke wide from midfield into forward positions to compensate for the absence of wingers. This style of play set a trend for many years despite the fact that great stamina is needed to play the 4.3.3 system.

Q *How important do you think it is to have a good relationship with the press?*

A Absolutely crucial. Especially when you know that the news is going to be relayed all over the world. You come to recognise the reporters whom you can trust, and you avoid those who are merely looking for sensationalism and headline stories. When you know that your family are reading the newspapers back at home it makes you realise the importance of accurate stories.

Q *Is it an advantage to have played in Europe when it comes to playing in the World Cup?*

A Yes it is, because the European game is slower than its English counterpart. For example, when I played in Sweden, the players were very skilful and they managed to slow the game down to their own pace. International football is much less frenetic than our own players are used to. Fortunately, many of our English players have some form of European experience which I am sure will be beneficial to them in 1990.

Q *Which of your present and past team-mates at Hearts and Newcastle United are likely to make the grade at international level, in your opinion?*

A Scott Crabbe, David Kirkwood and Alan McClaren of Hearts, Lee Clark and Tommy Heron of Newcastle. Both clubs have a good youth policy and so they are likely to have an excellent team in four or five years' time, providing they hold on to the players.

Q *What are your future aspirations as an international player?*

A Mainly, the European Nations' Championship in 1992. However, there will be younger players arriving on the football scene, and I will then be thirty-four. All I can say is that if Billy Bingham needs me, I will play to the best of my abilities.

Q *In the years to come, how would you like to be remembered as a player?*

A I would be very happy if people could say of David McCreery, 'He never let anyone down; he tried his utmost and gave everything he had in each match he played.'

WORLD CUP SOCCER QUIZ

1   Where were the first Cup Finals held?

2   Whom did Uruguay beat in the 1930 World Cup Final?

3   Which was the first country to win the World Cup on foreign soil?

4   Whom did Italy beat in the 1938 Final in Paris?

5   Which country staged the first World Cup Finals after the last war?

6   West Germany beat Hungary 3–2 in the 1954 Final, but what was the score when the same countries met earlier in a group 2 match?

7   In what year did Brazil win their first World Cup?

8   Brazil won the Trophy in Chile in 1962. Whom did they beat in the Final?

9   Uruguay beat France 2–1 in group 1 in 1966. Where was the match played?

10 Who was the leading goal-scorer in those 1966 Finals?

11 Brazil beat Italy to record their third World Cup win in 1970. Whom did they beat in the semi-final?

12 West Germany won the Trophy in 1974, but could only finish second in their group. Who won this group?

13 Who finished in third place in those 1974 Finals?

14   Argentina won the 1978 Finals in their own country, but lost one match on the way. Who beat them?

15   Holland lost the 1978 Final in extra time. Which country was the only one to beat them at those Finals in normal time?

16   Which is the only 1990 qualifying country never to have been beaten at a World Cup Finals?

17   How many goals did England concede at the 1982 Finals in Spain?

18   Beaten finalists West Germany lost one game in the 1982 Finals. Who beat them?

19   In the 1986 Finals, two countries achieved maximum six points in their group. Brazil was one. Which was the other?

20   Which country won the third-place match at the 1986 Finals?

21   When did Wales last qualify for a World Cup Final?

22   With which country did Northern Ireland draw to qualify for the 1986 World Cup Finals?

23   Scotland lost 4–1 to Brazil in the 1982 World Cup Finals, but who scored the Scottish goal?

24   Can you name the country which denied Wales a place in the 1986 World Cup Finals?

25   Which former Manchester United player became the youngest person to play in the World Cup Finals?

26   Which former Ipswich player scored the goal that

beat Hungary at Wembley in 1981 to secure England a place in the 1982 World Cup Finals?

27 Gary Lineker was leading scorer in the 1986 World Cup Finals, but how many goals did he score?

28 England failed to reach the World Cup Finals in 1974 as a result of a 1–1 draw against Poland at Wembley in 1973. Name the England scorer.

29 Whom did Bryan Robson succeed as England captain?

30 Who took over as England manager directly after the sacking of Alf Ramsey in 1974?

31 Northern Ireland beat the hosts of the 1982 World Cup in Valencia. Who were they, and which former Brighton player scored the goal?

32 Who played in France but sank the French national team with two goals in a World Cup qualifier in 1989?

33 How old was Dino Zoff when Italy won the 1982 World Cup?

34 Diego Maradona was sent off against which team in the 1982 World Cup Final?

Answers

1. Uruguay
2. Argentina
3. Italy
4. Hungary
5. Brazil
6. Hungary 8 West Germany 3
7. 1958
8. Czechoslavakia
9. White City
10. Eusebio – 9
11. Uruguay
12. East Germany
13. Poland
14. Italy
15. Scotland
16. Cameroon
17. 1
18. Algeria
19. Denmark
20. France
21. 1958
22. England
23. David Narey
24. Scotland
25. Norman Whiteside
26. Paul Mariner
27. 6
28. Allan Clarke
29. Ray Wilkins
30. Joe Mercer
31. Spain –
32. Mo Johnston
33. 41
34. Brazil

ITALY, 1990

The opening game of the 52-match Finals series will begin in Milan at 5.00 pm (British time) on Friday 8 June 1990. Argentina, as defending champions, will be playing Cameroon in this match. The Finals tournament extends to 31 days, two more than the 1986 Finals in Mexico.

Teams are arranged in six groups of four. In each group the teams play each other once and a league table is drawn up from the results. The champions and runners-up from each group, together with the four best third-placed teams, make the sixteen teams for a knock-out competition covering the second round, quarter-finals and semi-finals. The four semi-finalists contest a place in the World Cup Final or the third- and fourth-place play-off. The winner of the Final will be world champions and qualify automatically for the 1994 competition in the United States of America.

Preparations for this year's competition began several years ago as soon as the venue was announced. Decisions were made regarding the towns which would host the games and the improvements necessary for players, spectators and journalists alike. The 1990 World Cup,

---

AMAZING FACT

Dino Zoff (Italy) made his 100th appearance against Poland in the 1982 series.

---

in contrast to that held in 1930, will be shown live on television throughout the world via satellite, and stadia will have to house commentary boxes and television studios as well as increased seating capacity for spectators. Millions of lire have already been spent on improved car parking, lighting and security within and around the football grounds.

In order to recover the costs and, with any luck, make a profit, there is extensive merchandising of the tournament. Most people think that the expenditure is worth while because the souvenir trade, in particular, prospers from this boom period. Spain in 1982 issued commemorative stamps, and even set up an official travel agency to take care of the needs of foreign visitors. The Italians themselves, through their soccer pools, voted for the name of their mascot – Bimbo – a stylised figure of a soccer player in the Italian national colours of red, green and white, with a football for a head.

Italian officials have said that strict controls and identity checks were agreed with the English Football Association, to prevent known hooligans from obtaining tickets for the competition. All people buying tickets in Italy, allowed only through the biggest state banks, had to show identity documents and were given vouchers to be exchanged for tickets in May, allowing time for police checks.

It is not only English hooliganism that is worrying the Italian authorities, with bad reputations growing in other countries including their own. In 1989, leading Italian soccer players said that they were prepared to strike and call a halt to their league championship, in a dramatic move against escalating fan violence – a move prompted by the outbursts of hooliganism which saw two people die in soccer-related violence last season as rival fans clashed almost weekly in Milan, Rome, Verona, Bologna and Florence.

There is always heavy pressure on the host team to win the competition, and this year is no exception. The Italian coach, Azeglio Vicini, has attempted to take some pressure off his country by tipping the Brazilians as one of the teams for the Final. The form of the Brazilians has rarely been inspirational until recently, but after watching the Samba specialists win the South American Championship, Vicini admitted: 'I hope that we do not have to meet Brazil in next year's Finals. They

---

AMAZING FACT

The highest average number of goals scored in a Finals tournament is 5.3 per game in 1954. The lowest is 2.5 in 1974 and 1986. The highest aggregate of attendances is 2,199,941 in 1986, and the highest average crowd per game is 60,772 in Brazil in 1950.

---

look good again, with a blend of young and old players, and they have adapted well to new European-style tactics, just as Argentina did in the last World Cup.'

As a look at the list of participating countries shows, there are several realistic contenders apart from Brazil and Italy, and the scene is set for a close-run competition. History has shown that great teams are formed from a core of very talented players. Just look at some of the most outstanding teams since the war. The dazzlingly gifted Hungarian side of the 1950s had Puskas, Bozsik, Toth, Hidegkuti and Kocsis. The Brazilians of 1958 and 1962 had Gilmar in goal, and forwards such as Didì, Pelé, and the greatest of dribblers Garrincha, not to mention Zagalo. The England team in 1966 had a superb goalkeeper in Banks, a fearless defender in Bobby Moore, and in Bobby Charlton a midfield player of tremendous skills. The Brazilian team in 1970 boasted a Pelé of peerless ability, and to partner him they had found a midfield player of craft and poise in Gerson and an attacker of lightning speed in Jairzinho, the only player to have scored in every match at every stage in a World Cup Finals tournament. The team from West Germany in 1974 possessed a captain of class in Beckenbauer, a striker of menace in Muller, and a hard-working player in Overath.

In making your predictions for 1990, analyse the

┌─ *AMAZING FACT* ─────────────────────────

The Brazilians share their three wins with Italy, the Italians having been successful in 1934, 1938 and 1982. Uruguay, West Germany and Argentina have two wins each. The Uruguayans were winners in 1930 and 1950; West Germany in 1954 and 1974; the Argentinians in 1978 and 1986. England won in 1966.

└──

teams in terms of individual skills such as those of the Brazilian Bebeto, nicknamed the 'new Zico' when he exploded on the international scene; Italy's top striker, Gianluca Vialli; Holland's Ruud Gullit and Marco van Basten; England's Lineker and Waddle; and, of course, the irrepressible Argentinian Diego Maradona.

Millions of people will be glued to their sets watching 'The Greatest Show on Earth'. The performances of some of the international stars will guarantee that they become household names for years to come. Let us hope above all that the World Cup Finals are a credit to everyone who takes part. There will probably be some incidents with so many different nations and temperaments involved, but hopefully we will all remember the glorious moments, of which there are bound to be very many, when the history books are written.

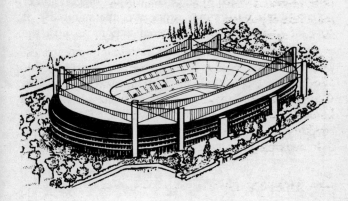

THE UNITED STATES OF AMERICA, 1994

The 1994 World Cup will be held in the USA. FIFA, the sport's governing body, chose the United States rather than Brazil and Morocco to stage the tournament. As well as being a money-spinning bonanza likely to rival the 1984 Los Angeles Olympics in terms of financial success, the 1994 competition will provide a major boost to the development of soccer in the States.

The decision means that the Americans automatically qualify for the competition, as host nation. The United States' bid included a videotaped message from ex-President Ronald Reagan in which he said that the USA would be honoured to stage the world's biggest soccer event. While purists may argue over the suitability of one of soccer's last unconquered nations to host the

four-yearly showpiece, the decision to hold the Finals in the States will, undeniably, stimulate the growth of the game in that country.

Authorities in the United States have already started planning for the World Cup, and they have tremendous facilities including all-seated stadia. Soccer was the most successful event at the 1984 Olympics in Los Angeles, pulling in crowds of over 80,000.

All qualifying matches for the 1994 World Cup will have to be played before all-seated crowds, a ruling made by FIFA in July 1989 when their executive committee announced that fans will not be allowed to stand at any matches, including both qualifying games and the Finals. With Wembley due to become all-seated next spring, this should pose no special problem for England but will have implications for several other prospective participants.

AMAZING FACT

The highest score in a qualifying game was achieved during the 1982 series when New Zealand beat Fiji 13–0. The Kiwis actually played 15 matches on the way to reaching the Finals. Goalkeeper Richard Wilson completed 15 hours 20 minutes without conceding a goal.

WORLD CUP 1990 – THE FINALS

In addition to the twenty-two countries that reached Italy via the qualifying rounds. Italy, as hosts, and Argentina, as holders, were given automatic entry to the Finals.

For the Finals the teams are organised into six groups of four teams each. The matches of each group will be played at two venues each (see the map on the facing page).

From each group the top two teams will qualify for the knock-out stages of the tournament. In addition the four best third-placed teams will qualify; these will be decided on points and goal difference.

The Groups

Group A
● *Rome & Florence*
Italy (seeded)
Austria
United States
Czechoslovakia

Group B
● *Naples & Bari*
Argentina (seeded)
Cameroon
USSR
Romania

Group C
● *Turin & Genoa*
Brazil (seeded)
Sweden
Costa Rica
Scotland

Group D
● *Milan & Bologna*
West Germany (seeded)
Yugoslavia
United Arab Emirates
Columbia

Group E
● *Verona & Udine*
Belgium (seeded)
South Korea
Uruguay
Spain

Group F
● *Cagliari & Palermo*
England (seeded)
Republic of Ireland
Holland
Egypt

Group A

Matches

June 9th (8pm) – Rome
Italy 1 v 0 **Austria**

June 10th (4pm) – Florence
USA 1 v 5 **Czechoslovakia**

June 14th (8pm) – Rome
Italy 1 v 0 **USA**

June 15th (4pm) – Florence
Austria 0 v 1 **Czechoslovakia**

June 19th (8pm) – Rome
Italy __ v __ **Czechoslovakia**

June 19th (8pm) – Florence
Austria __ v __ **USA**

Final table

	P	W	D	L	F	A	Pts
1							
2							
3							
4							

Qualifying teams

1 _____
2 _____
3 _____

Team strip

Austria   Czechoslovakia   Italy   USA

Group B

Matches

June 8th (5pm) – Milan

Argentina 0 **v** 1 **Cameroon**

June 9th (4pm) – Bari

USSR 0 **v** 2 **Romania**

June 13th (8pm) – Naples

Argentina 2 **v** 0 **USSR**

June 14th (4pm) – Bari

Cameroon 2 **v** 1 **Romania**

June 18th (8pm) – Naples

Argentina 1 **v** 1 **Romania**

June 18th (8pm) – Bari

Cameroon 0 **v** 4 **USSR**

Final table

	P	W	D	L	F	A	Pts
1							
2							
3							
4							

Qualifying teams

1 _____
2 _____
3 _____

Team strip

Argentina   Cameroon   Romania   USSR

183

Group C

Matches

June 10th (8pm) – Turin

Brazil 2 v 1 **Sweden**

June 11th (4pm) – Genoa

Costa Rica 1 v 0 **Scotland**

June 16th (4pm) – Turin

Brazil __ v __ **Costa Rica**

June 16th (8pm) – Genoa

Sweden __ v __ **Scotland**

June 20th (8pm) – Turin

Brazil 1 v 0 **Scotland**

June 20th (8pm) – Genoa

Sweden 1 v 2 **Costa Rica**

Final table	P	W	D	L	F	A	Pts
1							
2							
3							
4							

Qualifying teams

1 _____

2 _____

3 _____

Team strip

Brazil   Costa Rica   Scotland   Sweden

Group D

Matches   June 9th (8pm) – Bologna
             UAE 0 **v** 2 **Columbia**

             June 10th (8pm) – Milan
      West Germany 4 **v** 1 **Yugoslavia**

             June 14th (4pm) – Bologna
      Yugoslavia 1 **v** 0 **Columbia**

             June 15th (8pm) – Milan
      West Germany 5 **v** 1 **UAE**

             June 19th (4pm) – Milan
      West Germany 1 **v** 1 **Columbia**

             June 19th (4pm) – Bologna
        Yugoslavia __ **v** __ **UAE**

Final table	P	W	D	L	F	A	Pts
1							
2							
3							
4							

Qualifying teams

1 _____
2 _____
3 _____

Team strip

Columbia   UAE   West Germany   Yugoslavia

Group E

Matches

June 12th (4pm) – Verona

Belgium   ☂   v   ☁   **South Korea**

June 13th (4pm) – Udine

Uruguay   ☁   v   ☁   **Spain**

June 17th (8pm) – Verona

Belgium   ☂   v   ⊥   **Uruguay**

June 17th (8pm) – Udine

South Korea   __   v   __   **Spain**

June 21st (4pm) – Verona

Belgium   __   v   __   **Spain**

June 21st (4pm) – Udine

South Korea   __   v   __   **Uruguay**

Final table	P	W	D	L	F	A	Pts
1							
2							
3							
4							

Qualifying teams

1 _____

2 _____

3 _____

Team strip

Belgium   South Korea   Spain   Uruguay

Group F

Matches

June 11th (8pm) – Cagliari

England ⌞ v ⌞ **Rep. of Ireland**

June 12th (8pm) – Palermo

Holland ⌞ v ⌞ **Egypt**

June 16th (8pm) – Cagliari

England 0 v 0 **Holland**

June 17th (4pm) – Palermo

Rep. of Ireland — v — **Egypt**

June 21st (8pm) – Cagliari

England ⌞ v 0 **Egypt**

June 21st (8pm) – Palermo

Rep. of Ireland 0 v 0 **Holland**

Final table

	P	W	D	L	F	A	Pts
1							
2							
3							
4							

Qualifying teams

1 England
2 Rep of Ireland
3 Holland

Team strip

Egypt   England   Holland   Rep. of Ireland

Second round matches

June 23rd – Naples

Winner of Group B   **Third place in A, C or D**

_____ — v — _____

– Bari

Second in Group A   **Second in Group C**

_____ — v — _____

June 24th – Turin

Winner of Group C   **Third place in A, B or F**

_____ — v — _____

– Milan

Winner of Group D   **Third place in B, E or F**

_____ — v — _____

June 25th – Rome

Winner of Group A   **Third place in C, D or E**

_____ — v — _____

– Genoa

Second in Group F   **Second in Group B**

_____ — v — _____

June 26th – Bologna

Winner of Group F   **Second in Group E**

_____ — v — _____

– Verona

Winner of Group E   **Second in Group D**

_____ — v — _____

Quarter-finals

June 30th – Rome

Winner of match in Rome	Winner of match in Genoa
——————— — v —	———————

– Florence

Winner of match in Verona	Winner of match in Turin
——————— — v —	———————

July 1st – Naples

Winner of match in Naples	Winner of match in Bologna
——————— — v —	———————

– Milan

Winner of match in Milan	Winner of match in Bari
——————— — v —	———————

Semi-finals

July 3rd – Naples

Winner of match in Florence	Winner of match in Rome
——————— — v —	———————

July 4th – Turin

Winner of match in Milan	Winner of match in Naples
——————— — v —	———————

Third-Place match

July 7th – Bari

——————— — v — ———————

The 1990 World Cup Final

July 8th – Rome

Teams

West germany v _0 Argentina_

Players

No.	_Name_	No.	_Name_
___	_____	___	_____
___	_____	___	_____
___	_____	___	_____
___	_____	___	_____
___	_____	___	_____
___	_____	___	_____
___	_____	___	_____
___	_____	___	_____
___	_____	___	_____
___	_____	___	_____
___	_____	___	_____

Substitutes

No.	_Name_	No.	_Name_
___	_____	___	_____
___	_____	___	_____
___	_____	___	_____
___	_____	___	_____

Scorers

_____   _____

_____   _____

Referee _____

Linesmen _____   _____

World Champions 1990

_____

Statistics

Who and where

Series	Winning Country	Winning Captain	Winning Manager
1930	Uruguay	Jose Nasazzi	Odino Viera
1934	Italy	Giampiero Combi	Vittorio Pozzo
1938	Italy	Guiseppe Meazza	Vittorio Pozzo
1950	Uruguay	Obdulio Varela	Colonel Volpe
1954	W. Germany	Fritz Walter	Sepp Herberger
1958	Brazil	Hilderaldo Bellini	Vicente Feola
1962	Brazil	Ramos de Oliviera Maura	Aymore Moreira
1966	England	Bobby Moore	Alf Ramsey
1970	Brazil	Carlos Alberto	Mario Zagalo
1974	W. Germany	Franz Beckenbauer	Helmut Schoen
1978	Argentina	Daniel Passarella	Cesar Luis Menotti
1982	Italy	Dino Zoff	Enzo Bearzot
1986	Argentina	Diego Maradona	Carlos Bilardo
1990			

Leading scorers

Series	Player(s)	Country	Games	Goals
1930	Guillermo Stabile	Argentina	4	8
1934	Angelo Schiavio	Italy*	4	4
	Oldrich Nejedly	Czechoslovakia	4	4
	Edmund Conen	Germany	4	4
1938	Da Silva Leonidas	Brazil	4	8
1950	Marques Ademir	Brazil*	6	7
1954	Sandor Kocsis	Hungary	5	11
1958	Just Fontaine	France	6	13
1962	Drazen Jerkovic	Yugoslavia	6	5

1966	Ferreira Eusebio	Portugal	6	9
1970	Gerd Muller	W. Germany	6	10
1974	Grzegorz Lato	Poland	7	7
1978	Mario Kempes	Argentina*	7	6
1982	Paolo Rossi	Italy*	7	6
1986	Gary Lineker	England	5	6
1990				

*= *winning country*

Averages

Series	Venue	Matches	Attendances Total	Ave.	Goals Total	Ave.
1930	Uruguay	18	434,500	24,139	70	3.88
1934	Italy	17	395,000	23,235	70	4.11
1938	France	18	483,000	26,833	84	4.66
1950	Brazil	22	1,337,000	60,772	88	4.00
1954	Switzerland	26	943,000	36,270	140	5.38
1958	Sweden	35	868,000	24,800	126	3.60
1962	Chile	32	776,000	24,250	89	2.78
1966	England	32	1,614,677	50,458	89	2.78
1970	Mexico	32	1,673,975	52,312	95	2.96
1974	W. Germany	38	1,774,022	46,685	97	2.55
1978	Argentina	38	1,610,215	42,374	102	2.68
1982	Spain	52	1,766,277	33,967	146	2.81
1986	Mexico	52	2,285,498	43,952	132	2.54
1990	Italy					